Fr

Book #1

The Rebels

By Elianna Wylie

Wylie Books
Canada

This book is dedicated to my Mom, who made it possible.

The Rebels
Second edition

Cover illustration by Elianna Wylie

ISBN 978-1-7778433-0-4

Wylie Books
4 Chesterton Lane
Guelph, Ontario, Canada
N1E 6T1

Chapter 1

Gunshots. The Nazis. They were found!

"Run!" someone called.

"But our supplies! They will be lost!"

"Take what you can and run!"

Pearl saw all the rushing and was afraid. Her mentor said their base could never be found! It was too well hidden. But even as she thought this she realized: the Nazis would always find us.

"Pearl run!"

Pearl looked around and realized that almost all of the Rebels had left. Quickly, she grabbed some supplies and ran, following the rest of the Rebels. Then, she heard the sound of men behind her. Quickly, she put on an extra burst of speed and ran like the wind, hoping to lose the Nazis in the undergrowth. Finally, when the Rebels could no longer hear their pursuers, their leader, Viper Strike, called for a rest, and Pearl walked over to her mentor, Wolf Eye.

"Wolf Eye, tell me again how you got your warrior name!"

"Not now, Pearl."

"Please? It would help me get my mind off - off what happened."

"Oh, alright." Wolf Eye sighed. "But before I begin, don't forget that you don't have to do a great feat like I did to get a warrior name. You can get a warrior name for a skill that you have, after I have taught you everything you need to know."

"I know, Wolf Eye. Now can you get to the story?"

"Yes, yes, I was just getting to that. It was many years ago, and we were trying to blow up a train that was taking supplies to the Nazis. We had a guard posted every night, and we were sure that no one was aware of our presence. But one day, about halfway into the journey, I saw something flicking through the trees. Moments later, I realized that we were being followed. Quickly, I told the mission's leader, Bear Strength, and we were able to fight them off. Thanks to me, we were able to successfully carry out the mission. Once we got back, Viper Strike gave me my warrior name, Wolf Eye, after the keen eye of a wolf."

Then Viper Strike called, "Come on! We need to find a safe place by nightfall."

No one argued, even Talon Claw, who was known for his grumpy attitude. Once they set off, the warriors started talking amongst themselves and Pearl, looking for a distraction, wandered over to the other apprentices.

"I can't believe it was found!" Mike was saying. He was a fairly old recruit, and was known for his sharp mind and good ideas.

"Yeah, I keep expecting for us to turn around and go back." Asher agreed. Usually Asher was joking around, but today he was dead serious. That really showed how scared he was.

"I know, it's so sad," said Pearl.

"My mentor is devastated. She lost almost half her pearls, and it's really hard to get them these days." That was Lily, the apprentice of Jewel Crafter. Jewel Crafter used pearls to make stronger and faster weapons. The job requires great skill and focus, both of which Lily had.

"Almost half?" Pearl cried. "But we need them more than ever now!"

"For revenge," said Lucas.

Pearl had heard a little about Lucas's past, and knew that he had lost all of his family and friends to the Nazis, and so was bent on revenge. Even after hearing again and again all of the terrible things the Nazis had done, she still could barely believe that some people could do that to others. It was horrible.

"How's this?" called Hawk Wing, a warrior and Asher's mentor.

They had come to a small, enclosed clearing. The conditions of the forest were just right for defending, because they could see for a good distance on all sides. Unfortunately, that meant that they would be easily seen if anyone came close enough, but it was good for now.

"Good enough," Viper Strike said. "Wolf Eye, Jewel Crafter, Goat Jump, help me guard. The rest of you should get some sleep."

Pearl started to daydream. Goat Jump was a great cook. In better times, when they had lots of food, he would cook meals that practically sang with flavors. Pearl sighed. How she wished that the Nazis had not found them. How she wished everything would go back to normal.

"Pearl! It's time to sleep!" Wolf Eye called.

*　　　*　　　*

Pearl was settling down and was almost asleep, when…

"Ow! Ow, ow, ow!"

Pearl sighed, recognizing the voice. "What is it Asher?"

"I think I sprained my ankle!"

"I'll get Magic Healer."

After a brief examination, Magic Healer announced, "You're fine. All you did was stub your toe."

"But it hurts like crazy!"

"You're fine. Now get some sleep."

Pearl rolled over, and hoped that this time she would get to sleep without interruptions.

* * *

The next day they set off, with Asher in the lead.

"Thought you sprained your ankle," Pearl teased, as Asher jumped over a log.

"It's all better now."

"Good to hear that."

The other apprentices laughed.

"Lily!" Jewel Crafter called.

"Got to go, Jewel Crafter's calling me," Lily said regretfully.

"Okay. See you!" Lucas said.

One by one, they said goodbye and went to their mentors: Lily to Jewel Crafter, Asher to Hawk Wing, Pearl to Wolf Eye, Mike to Goat Jump, and Lucas to Vine Hang. Vine Hang is a good natured warrior who can zip through tree tops like the wind. Although he helped cook sometimes, it was only because all the other warriors, besides Goat Jump, were even worse cooks than him. At least they had Goat Jump.

Pearl walked over to Wolf Eye. "What are we doing for training today?"

"Well, I thought that we could do some sword moves."

"Okay!"

They walked a little ways away from the Rebels, when they heard some soft, sad, mewing.

"That sounds like kittens!" Pearl exclaimed. "Can we check it out?"

"Okay, but be careful."

"I will!"

They walked silently to the source of the sound. And there, tucked into a bush, were two kittens! They were so young that they hadn't opened their eyes yet.

"Can I keep them?" Pearl asked.

"I don't know, we have to ask Viper Strike."

"Okay!"

Pearl ran out of the bushes. Wolf Eye sighed and followed.

* * *

"Viper Strike! Viper Strike!" Pearl yelled.

"What is it Pearl?"

"Me and Wolf Eye found some kittens and he said if you said I could I can keep them!"

"Slow down Pearl. What was that again?"

"When we were out training, Wolf Eye and I found some kittens! Can I keep them?"

"Well, if you take complete care of them, and that care doesn't get in the way of your training, then I don't see why not."

"Thank you, thank you, thank you!"

Viper Strike laughed. "Come on, go show your kittens to me."

"Okay!" Pearl raced off towards the kittens.

"Hawk Wing, you're in charge!" Viper Strike called.

"Yippee! My mentor's in charge!" exclaimed Asher.

"Asher," Hawk Wing warned.

Before anymore was said, Viper Strike followed Pearl into the forest.

Chapter 2

Following the trail left in Pearl's wake, Viper Strike and Wolf Eye chatted.

"You haven't shown her how to hide her trail yet, have you?" Viper Strike asked.

"No, but even if I did, she wouldn't remember it right now."

"Probably not."

* * *

"The kittens are here!" Pearl called, just as Viper Strike and Wolf Eye caught up to her.

"Aren't they cute? Thank you so much for letting me keep them!" Pearl said excitedly.

"You're welcome. Now let's get them back to camp," Viper Strike responded.

"Okay!"

* * *

After setting down the kittens in a soft nest of clothes and blankets, Pearl went to Wolf Eye to finish the training session.

"Change of plans for this session," Wolf Eye said. "I will teach you how to hide your trail."

"Okay!"

"Hiding your trail is vital for any mission. It allows you to sneak into places without leaving a trace."

"I know that!"

"Well, now you got to learn it. Come on, now."

*   *   *

They practiced until lunch.

"You're better than before, but definitely not the best," Wolf Eye commented as Pearl, almost stealthily, crept through the undergrowth.

"You need to watch out for twigs though," he continued as Pearl stepped on a twig. "They're like burglar alarms."

“Okay, Wolf Eye. Let’s get back to camp.”

“Alright. Wanting to see your kittens?”

“Of course!”

“Well don’t let me stop you, but don’t forget to eat lunch!”

“I won't!”

Just before they reached camp, they heard something. Crouching in some bushes, they waited in tense silence. Then,

“Come on out Asher. You should know better than sneaking up on people like that, especially after what happened to the base.” Wolf Eye reprimanded.

“But it was funny!” Asher protested.

“No it was not. Hawk Wing will be hearing about this.”

“But he will confine me to camp!”

“And that’s what he should do. Now back to camp, both of you.”

* * *

After getting to camp, Wolf Eye went over to Hawk Wing to tell him what Asher had done, while Pearl was checking on her kittens. Asher went with her.

"I'm in for it," Asher groaned. "I won't be able to explore for a week!"

"Two weeks actually," said Hawk Wing, coming up behind them.

"Come on!" Asher groaned.

"You deserve it Asher." Hawk Wing said. "I thought I trained you better than this."

"Can we continue this when my friend is not around?" Asher asked.

"Alright. Meet me here after lunch, or else three weeks of no exploration," Hawk Wing warned.

"Okay," Asher agreed.

Pearl said goodbye to her kittens, and Asher and Pearl went to get lunch, and talk to the other apprentices about Asher's demise.

"Asher, I would think even you would know better than to do that!" Lily exclaimed, after the story had been told.

"Please don't give me a talking to," Asher asked. "I already got one from Wolf Eye and one from Hawk Wing is coming up."

Lily laughed. “Oh, alright.”

“I think it was kind of funny,” Lucas said.

“You wouldn’t if you weren’t allowed to explore for two weeks!” Asher protested.

“True,” Lucas agreed.

“Hey Lily, how long do you think Jewel Crafter’s pearls will last?” Pearl asked.

“I don’t know. Three or four months, if we’re lucky.” Lily answered.

“And if we’re not?” Mike asked.

“Then a month or two, but I don't think it will come to that.” Lily said.

“I didn’t realize we were that low. Do you think we could get some from the old base?” Lucas asked.

“No. it would be too well guarded, and besides, the Nazis would have taken them all anyways," Mike said.

“Right.” Lucas agreed.

“Come on, let’s eat, not talk. I’m starving!” Asher said.

“Alright Asher, alright.” Pearl laughed.

* * *

After chowing down on their food, they stayed to talk a bit.

"Can I have seconds?" Lucas asked.

"Sorry mate," Vine Hang said. "Only one serving."

Just then, Talon Claw passed by. "Youngsters these days never realize that their elders are people that eat too. When I was a kid, children had proper manners."

"Now, now, Talon Claw," Vine Hang said. "Lucas didn't know that we were short on food."

"Humph."

"Hey," Pearl interrupted. "Can I show you guys what I learned today?'

"I have to meet Hawk Wing," Asher groaned. "Thanks though."

The other apprentices, pleased for a distraction, went with Pearl.

Chapter 3

After an hour, the apprentices were called off for training, and Pearl went to see her kittens.

“Hi cuties! Do you want some milk?”

“Meow!”

“I take that as a yes!”

Pearl fed the kittens through an old can she was using as a bottle and sang to them until they went to sleep.

“Good-night, kitties.”

Then, she walked over to where a meager dinner was being served.

“What is there?” Pearl asked.

“Spinach and pig’s feet,” Goat Jump replied.

“Oh, uh, okay," Pearl stuttered. It did not sound appetizing.

After picking out the least-gross looking items, she walked over to the other apprentices.

“Can you believe it? Spinach and pig’s feet! Pig’s feet! I didn’t even know we had that!” Asher complained.

"At least we have something Asher. Some of the warriors are going hungry just to keep us fed." Lily said.

"What!" Pearl exclaimed, shocked.

"It's true. We are younger, so we should be fed." said Lily.

"Oh well. More for me!" Asher joked.

"Asher. Not funny." Lucas said.

"Hey! That's not nice!" Asher protested.

"Well, it's true." Lucas argued.

"Asher, Lucas, stop it. We don't need a fight on top of everything else." Lily reprimanded.

"Fine." Lucas agreed sulkily.

"Oh, alright," Asher said. "But only because Lucas is doing it too."

*   *   *

They finished their dinner, with minimal gagging, said goodnight, and settled down for sleep.

Then, just as Pearl was almost asleep, she heard the warriors talking in hushed whispers.

"We need to find a good location soon," Viper Strike said.

"These kids don't stand a second in the wild." Talon Claw grumbled. "Back in my days-"

"Not now, Talon Claw. We can't waste time with your grumblings." Viper Strike said.

"Humph."

"Back to business." Viper Strike ordered. "Any ideas?"

"We should send out scouts to look for potential bases," Wolf Eye suggested.

"Good idea, Wolf Eye. We will send out scouts at midday tomorrow." Viper Strike said. "Now rest."

Pearl heard the warriors setting down. Pretty soon the only things she could hear was the rustle of leaves and mews of her kittens. Her kittens! Quickly and quietly, Pearl made her way over to them. She gave them some milk she had saved, and rocked them till they fell asleep. Then, she crept back to her makeshift bed.

"I wonder if Wolf Eye will be a scout. If he is, I hope I can go with him," Pearl thought as she drifted off to sleep.

Chapter 4

The next day when she woke up, the camp was filled with activity, as the scouts prepared for their journey. As Pearl had hoped, Wolf Eye was among them. Going over to him, she asked, "Wolf Eye, can I come with you?"

"I don't know. What about your kittens?" he asked.

"They can come with us!"

"What about their food?"

"I can carry it."

"As well as your own supplies? It will be heavy, and I won't be able to help you."

"I can do it!"

"Well, if you really want to go, then check with Viper Strike."

"Okay!"

Excited, Pearl ran over to Viper Strike.

"Viper Strike?" Pearl asked.

"What is it Pearl?" Viper Strike answered.

"Can I go with Wolf Eye?"

"It will be a hard journey, and the scouts are taking on a big risk. They can encounter many dangers. Besides, what about your kittens?"

"I can take them with me, and carry their supplies, as well as my own!"

"It would be heavy, and Wolf Eye wouldn't be able to help you."

"I can hold it!"

"What of the risks? It will be dangerous."

"Every second we live with Hitler as ruler is dangerous, so it is no different."

"True.

But it will be even more dangerous."

"I will be with Wolf Eye! And it will be a good experience for me! Don't you want that?"

"You are right, it is good for apprentices to get experience on explorations, and Wolf Eye went on one way more dangerous than this when he was your age. Very well, you may go, but be careful, and do everything Wolf Eye tells you."

"I will! Thank you Viper Strike!"

"You're welcome. Now go pack."

Pearl ran over to Wolf Eye.

"I can come! I can come!"

"Are your kittens coming?"

"Yes!"

"Very well. Get packed. We are leaving at midday, and if you aren't ready, you get left behind."

"Okay, Wolf Eye."

Pearl had a quick breakfast, then scurried around, getting her and her kitten's things backed.

"Where are you going?" Mike asked, coming over to her.

"I'm going scouting with Wolf Eye!" Pearl replied.

"Cool! Good luck!"

"Thanks!"

Pearl gathered the last of her things and ran over to Wolf Eye.

"I'm ready!" she exclaimed.

"And just in time. Let's go. We can eat lunch on the way."

They set off into the woods.

"What are we looking for?" Pearl asked.

"Hidden caves or hollows. It needs to be big enough for all of the Rebels and our supplies to fit in comfortably," Wolf Eye replied.

"Okay!"

*　　　*　　　*

The days swept by. They had run out of milk for the kittens, and so Pearl ground up squirrel guts for them to eat. They had found a few caves and hollow trees, but none of them were big enough to shelter the Rebels.

In their third week of traveling, Wolf Eye started a conversation, unusual for them, because usually they saved all of their energy for their trip.

"What are you going to name your kittens?" he asked.

"I don't know. I'm just waiting for the right names to come to me," Pearl said.

"Maybe you could name them after jewels, like your name," Wolf Eye suggested.

"I'll think about it."

Just then, they came upon a large tree growing in soft soil, in a clearing that was hidden by the dense foliage.

“What’s this?” Pearl asked.

“I don’t know. Go check it out if you want, but be careful!”

“I will! Watch my kittens please!”

Pearl scrambled up into the tree.

“There’s a hole big enough to fit a warrior comfortably down!” she reported, and clambered into it.

“Well that’s promising. Anything else?”

“I don't know. Hand me a torch please.”

“Hear you go.”

Wolf Eye carefully lowered down the flaming torch, careful not to catch the inside of the tree on fire.

“Be careful,” he warned. “As soon as this flame touches the tree, this place is done for.”

“I will.”

Heeding Wolf Eye’s warning, Pearl kept the torch a careful distance away from the walls while examining them. In its light, she could see that the inside of the tree ended in the soft soil that she had seen outside. Pushing her hand against the soil, it gave away easily.

“The soil would be easy to dig away. If there is a lot of this soft soil, we could easily make an underground city.” she reported.

“I think if none of the other scouts have found anything better, we may have found the new Rebel’s base!” Wolf Eye exclaimed.

“And I am the one that found it!”

Chapter 5

After Pearl clambered out, they made a makeshift covering for the hole. They decided to stay the night before starting back to the Rebels. Pearl stayed by the tree and collected berries and nuts to eat while Wolf Eye searched around for a stream. He brought back some water, then Pearl went to it to clean the grit of travel off her.

The next day, they had a quick breakfast, then started back to the Rebels, Pearl elated by their discovery.

Just before they left, Wolf Eye walked around the tree, glancing at the sun and looking around at the nearby landmarks.

“So we can find our way back,” he explained.

They travel for a few weeks, gathering nuts and berries to eat, and occasionally catching a few squirrels.

Pearl’s kittens weren’t really kittens anymore, they were hunting for themselves now, and Pearl didn't have to save the squirrel guts for them anymore. But even as they grew up, they still followed Pearl around, like devoted dogs.

They were getting close to camp on the third week of their return journey, and Wolf Eye was starting to recognize landmarks, when,

Crash!

Something was in the forest, and it didn't sound like an animal.

“Get down and keep your kittens quiet, Pearl,” Wolf Eye ordered.

Pearl, frightened, obeyed. They waited in tense silence. Then, voices.

“Those rebelling scum must be around here somewhere. Spread out and get to work.”

“Yes, sergeant!”

Through the trees, Pearl could see a patrol of Nazi soldiers. She could only hope they could not see her and Wolf Eye. As soon as the Nazis were gone, Wolf Eye turned to Pearl.

“Pearl, get to camp and warn the Rebels. I will try to slow them down.”

“But Wolf Eye-”

“Now Pearl,” Wolf Eye said in a voice that left no argument.

Pearl took off into the forest, putting all of the speed and stealth she had learned into her run. She ducked and dived, twisted and wove through the forest of trailing vines and branches. She heard a crack of a gun, but knew she could not turn back. The fate of the Rebels lay on her shoulders. Suddenly, she noticed the kittens were running beside her. But, she realized, they weren’t kittens anymore. They were cats, bigger and stronger than any house cat. They looked like Eurasian lynxes, though Pearl couldn't be sure. But whatever they were, Pearl felt comfort in that they were by her side.

Chapter 6

"The Nazis are coming! The Nazis are coming!" Pearl yelled, racing into camp.

"Where's Wolf Eye?" Viper Strike asked.

"Buying us time," Pearl replied.

"We should stay and fight!" Lucas said.

"No Lucas. We are too weak," Viper Strike argued.

"But we have nowhere to go!" Vine Hang protested.

"We should fight. The youngsters have a point," Talon Claw, in a rare moment of kindness, said.

Sighing, Viper Strike turned to Pearl. "How many are there?"

"Ten or twelve, I think." Pearl said.

"Alright, that is reasonable. We will fight. The Rebels! To arms!" Viper Strike ordered.

Everyone began scurrying around, picking weapons and getting to good defense locations. Pearl went over to the daggers, and picked two short ones. Her cats, sensing her fear, wove around her, comforting her.

"They're here!"

The fight was on. Soon the clearing was filled with the clang of swords, cracks of guns, and twangs of arrows. Pearl whirled around, disoriented. Then her lynxes guided her to the battle, and she was ready.

"Charge!" she yelled, and she and her cats surged forward, into the battle.

* * *

It was chaos. Pearl threw a dagger at a Nazi, and he ran off. Pearl grabbed the dagger and twirled around, looking for Rebels that were losing a fight. Hawk Wing and Vine Hang were chasing a Nazi into the forest, Talon Claw, despite his grumpy attitude, was a good fighter and was holding his own, Jewel Crafter, Magic Healer and Lily were back to back, and no Nazis were getting a hit in between their twirling swords. Asher, Mike, and Goat

Jump were in a circle together and were fine. That only left...

"Lucas!"

Looking around, Pearl spotted Lucas, surrounded by Nazis!

"Sundance! Moonlight! Attack them!" her cats followed her word, even though their names had only been thought up seconds ago. They rushed forward, trying to get to Lucas before the Nazis overwhelmed him. Running, Pearl saw her cats overtake her, throwing Lucas's attackers into the forest. The rest ran in fright of the two Eurasian lynxes. Lucas flashed a thumbs up to Pearl, then was swept away. But the battle was not over yet. Other Nazis had been alerted to the battle and were rushing in, and the Rebels were outnumbered. Desperately holding her own, Pearl heard a scream. It was Mike! She renewed her attack, trying to break through her attackers. But it was going to be too late....

Chapter 7

As Pearl watched, someone emerged through the trees, running towards Mike. As she looked closer, she realized it was Wolf Eye! His twirling swords kept the Nazis at bay long enough for Pearl and her cats to join the fight. Then, they were there. This fight was more intense than any other fight Pearl had been in yet. With slashing swords everywhere, she had to let her reflexes take over, guiding her through the battle. After Mike was safe, Pearl and her cats swept through the battle, until finally, the Nazis were gone, and everyone was bandaged up.

"We won!" Asher rejoiced.

"They know we are here though. We have to move immediately." Viper Strike ordered.

"But we have wounded!" Magic Healer protested.

"They must be healed on the way." Viper Strike ordered.

"But Wolf Eye can't travel!" Magic Healer protested again.

Wolf Eye was hurt! In the aftermath of the battle, Pearl hadn't realized that Wolf Eye had been wounded. Looking around, she saw him on a makeshift bed of moss and leaves, bandages all over.

"He will be carried. Hawk Wing, Talon Claw, will you do it?" Viper Strike asked.

"Of course," they both agreed.

"Good. Vine Hang, organize all patrols needed for the journey. Jewel Crafter can help you if it's too much." Viper Strike decided. "Scouts, what did you find on your journeys? The rest of the Rebels can return to your duties."

Pearl went first, and quickly told Viper Strike about the hollow tree she and Wolf Eye had found, then rushed over to Magic Healer.

"Will Wolf Eye be alright?" she asked.

"I don't know Pearl," Magic Healer responded wearily.

"But you can heal him right? You're the best healer!"

"Even the best healers can't heal everyone."

"But he's my mentor! I still need more training! No one could take his place!"

"I know you're upset Pearl. But I work better undisturbed, and besides, the Rebels need you. I promise to tell you right away if his condition changes, for better or for worse."

"Alright."

Pearl walked dejectedly to Vine Hang.

"What should I do?" Pearl asked.

"Gather up your cats for starters. We don't need them underfoot. Then pack up supplies with the rest of the apprentices," Vine Hang said.

"Okay. And Vine Hang?"

"Yes?"

"Do you think Wolf Eye will get better?"

"Of course he will. Don't worry."

"Magic Healer doesn't think so."

"She's just worried."

"I guess so."

Slowly, Pearl walked over to the other apprentices, who were chatting together while packing. The two lynxes trailed behind her.

"Hi Pearl!" The apprentices greeted her.

"Hi guys," Pearl responded wearily.

"Why are you so sad?" Lucas asked.

"Wolf Eye's hurt!" Pearl explained.

"Oh, that's too bad," Asher said.

"But you need to be strong," Lucas said. "For the Rebels."

"And we'll help you every step of the way, " Lily comforted.

"Thanks guys. I know I can count on you," Pearl said.

"Meow!" Sundance and Moonlight protested.

"And you too!" Pearl said with a laugh.

Just then, Viper Strike called out. "Let the Rebels gather!"

The apprentices walked over to her.

"It is time to leave. There were not many good locations found by our scouts, but Wolf Eye and Pearl brought back promising news. Because we cannot risk staying here to wait for more scouts, it is there we will head. Because Wolf Eye is injured, Pearl will have to lead us."

Pearl was surprised. "Me? But I'm only an apprentice!"

"Yes, but you and Wolf Eye are the only ones who know how to get there, and Wolf Eye is not fit to lead the journey," Viper Strike explained.

"Surely the other scouts found something better!" Pearl protested.

"No one found a better location than you two did."

"If there is no one else, then I will do it, for the good of the Rebels," Pearl decided.

"Good," Viper Strike said. "We will leave as soon as everyone is ready. Return to your duties, and come back as soon as you are ready."

The Rebels dispersed, getting the final things ready as Viper Strike had asked. Then, everyone was ready, and they were off.

Chapter 8

During the following days, Sundance and Moonlight were a great help. They remembered the trail by scent as well as sight, so if Pearl got lost they could lead the way. Not visibly though, because the rest of the Rebels were uneasy with the cats in their midst, and would not react well if they knew the cats were leading them, even if the cats were Pearl's.

After they had traveled for two weeks, they were getting low on protein, and they had to move too swiftly to spend hours on hunts that had only a chance at bringing back food. Then, during one of their lunch rests, Pearl had an idea.

"Sundance, Moonlight!" she called.

After they had come over to her, she asked the two lynxes, "Can you hunt for the Rebels? You do it every day for yourselves so it must not be hard."

The cats were getting strong and big off their hunting while the Rebels were getting thinner and thinner.

Meowing, the lynxes both nodded their heads, in what seemed to be agreement.

"Good," Pearl said. "Now be off! An ear scratch awaits you both when you come back!"

Then, both of the cats headed off. Just then, Jewel Crafter came up beside Pearl.

"Where did you send them?" she asked.

"Hunting for the Rebels," Pearl replied.

"Good idea."

Talon Claw was walking by, and heard this exchange.

"Not to me," he grumbled. "Relying on animals to bring us food! They could bring us poison!"

"Talon Claw, the food will be cooked and so even if there was poison then it would be cooked away," Jewel Crafter reasoned.

"There might be poisonous seeds that can't be cooked away," Talon Claw argued.

"The meat would be cleaned," Pearl reminded him.

Talon Claw could think of no further argument.

"See?" asked Jewel Crafter.

He huffed and stalked away.

"Oh Talon Claw, always grumpy. You can't blame him, he's lived through so much," Jewel Crafter said.

"Guess so. I'm going over to Wolf Eye. Bye!" Pearl said.

Jewel Crafter laughed. "Bye!"

Pearl ran over to Wolf Eye and Magic Healer.

"How is Wolf Eye?" she asked.

"Much better. He woke up earlier," Magic Healer said. "He's asleep now though."

"Why didn't you tell me?" Pearl asked. "I would have wanted to talk to him!"

"You were leading the Rebels. I didn't want to stop them just because Wolf Eye was awake. You know he hates being made a fuss of," Magic Healer said.

"Right. Well, next time he wakes up, tell him I said hi. Bye!"

"Bye Pearl."

Pearl was walking over to the apprentices when Viper Strike stopped her.

"Pearl, where are you cats?" Viper Strike asked.

"They're out hunting for the Rebels. I thought we could use the meat," Pearl said.

"Good thinking. The Rebels will benefit from you."

Pearl beamed. That was about the highest compliment you could get from Viper Strike. "Thanks," she said. "I'm just trying to help."

Then, they heard Hawk Wing calling Viper Strike from across the clearing.

"Got to go," Viper Strike said. "Maybe get something to eat and rest. You've been working hard."

"Alright Viper Strike."

Viper Strike walked away. Just then, Moonlight came running towards her, but she had no prey.

"Moonlight! I thought I told you to hunt!" Pearl exclaimed.

In response, Moonlight started pacing, as if she wanted to show Pearl something. Pearl looked across the clearing, and caught Vine Hang's eye.

"Vine Hang? Can you come with me?" she asked. "Moonlight wants to show me something but I don't want to go out without a warrior."

"Alright. I could use the distraction," he agreed. "Just make it quick."

Moonlight, seeing that they were coming, started padding into the forest, checking over her shoulder every few seconds to make sure that they were following. After a while, they heard Sundance purring. Pearl glanced at Vine Hang. Something was up. Sundance didn't purr to plants. Vine Hang motioned to be silent. Cautiously, they crept forward, and Pearl saw with surprise that Sundance was in a small clearing with what looked to be a small child! Sundance was comforting her, and Moonlight, after checking Vine Hang and Pearl were still there, went to join her. Pearl motioned for Vine Hang to stay back, and stepped into the clearing.

Chapter 9

"Who are you?" the child asked, frightened. Pearl realized she was a girl.

"I am Pearl, and these are my cats," Pearl responded. "What's your name?"

"Mary. My name is Mary," Mary said.

"Nice to meet you Mary. Why are you out here?"

"The Nazis. Our car crashed. They killed my family. They want to kill me too. They are hunting me. Are you going to hand me in?"

"No, we won't hand you in."

"We? You are with others?"

Pearl hadn't told Mary about the Rebels. "Yes. Vine Hang!"

Vine Hang came out of the forest. "So the Nazis are after you too? Join the gang," he said.

"Why are the Nazis hunting you? Did your car crash?" Mary asked.

"No," Pearl said. She glanced at Vine Hang, who gave an almost unperceivable shake of his head, signaling to her not to tell Mary that they were a part of the Rebels. But then what to tell her?

"Vine Hang, go tell the others about Mary. They can decide." Pearl commanded overconfidently.

"Decide what?" Mary asked.

Vine Hang ignored her. "Blind fold her, then go to camp and tell the others," he ordered.

"No," Pearl argued. "You should go to camp because I am the only one my cats answers to."

"How do you know that?" Vine Hang demanded. "No one's ever tried."

"Because no one can. Besides, don't forget I am the one that invited you, not the other way around, so I am in charge." Pearl argued.

"The warrior is always in charge," Vine Hang challenged.

"But you move faster in the trees," Pearl persisted.

Just then, Mary whimpered, scared. "What are you arguing about?"

"Oh, it's nothing," Pearl said. "Go on, Vine Hang, or you'll scare her more."

Grumbling, Vine Hang set off into the forest. “Viper Strike will hear about this!”

After Vine Hang left, Pearl turned to Mary. “Because we don't want the Nazis finding us, we take every precaution, so I will have to blindfold and pat you down, okay?”

“But I'm scared of the dark!” Mary protested.

“Light will still come in, you just won't be able to see where you are going.”

“Will the patting down be uncomfortable?”

“Don't think so.”

“Can the kitties lead me?”

“Sure.”

“How long will the journey take?”

“Twenty minutes or so,” Pearl responded, and started patting down Mary.

“Are they all grumps like Vine Hang?”

Pearl laughed. “Vine Hang isn't usually a grump. It’s Talon Claw you need to look out for.”

“Why do they have weird names and you don’t?”

“They’re warriors, and those names describe one of their skills.”

"So will you get one of those names?"

"Yes," Pearl finished patting down Mary and put a blindfold on her. "Now come on, you're ready."

* * *

They were almost at the clearing. They had been walking slowly, stopping every few minutes to twirl Mary around. They had made a kind of game out of it. When they stopped, Pearl would say 'time to twirl, princess,' and Mary would giggle and twirl for a few minutes. By the time they got back, a crowd had gathered, waiting for their arrival. At the front was Viper Strike, and she did not look pleased. Pearl quickly took off Mary's blindfold.

"Pearl, who is this?" Viper Strike asked.

"This is Mary, Viper Strike," Pearl said. "Sundance and Moonlight found her while they were out hunting. I checked to make sure there weren't any trackers or recorders on her, and blindfolded her while we were walking, and spun her around many times. They can't find our location through her, I promise."

"I am sure you took all of the necessary precautions. What I am worried about is how you ran off, with only one warrior, without telling anyone what you were doing, and brought back another person to care for when we are already struggling to survive."

Pearl looked down, ashamed. "Yes, Viper Strike."

"For now, escort this child to Magic Healer, then report to me. Understand?"

"Yes, Viper Strike."

Pearl took Mary to Magic Healer, as Viper Strike had ordered.

"I'm sorry to leave you, but Magic Healer will take good care of you," she said to Mary.

"Why can't you stay?" Mary asked.

"Viper Strike wants me to go to her, so I have to."

"Why can't I come with you?"

"The meeting is private."

"Can you come right after?"

"I will try, but Viper Strike might want

me to do something. I promise to come as soon as I can though."

"Okay."

Magic Healer had stayed silent during this, but now she spoke up. "Don't worry Mary, we will have fun together. Now run along Pearl, don't keep Viper Strike waiting."

"Okay," Pearl said. Sundance and Moonlight tried to follow her, but she told them to stay back. This meeting had no place for the two Eurasian lynxes.

She walked over to Viper Strike, a little afraid of what might happen. After a small nod, Viper Strike silently led Pearl to a deserted part of the clearing they were resting in.

"First of all Pearl," Viper Strike began, "you should know better than to leave the camp without alerting anyone, with so few people to protect you. It would always be a bad idea, but right now it is even worse, because you are our guide. If you got lost or killed, then we would be lost in the middle of nowhere until Wolf Eye is healed, and who knows how long that would take."

"But my cats can probably fight three warriors at once! There was no danger."

"That is not definite, and could they stand against fourteen Nazis?"

"Maybe."

"But that is not for sure. Secondly, you should not follow wild cats."

"Sundance and Moonlight aren't wild!"

"Even if they listen to you, they are still wild cats at heart, and would probably hurt the Rebels if it saved their hide."

"My cats-"

"Silence! I'm not done. You shouldn't take in people without my consent, even if you took all the necessary precautions. Taking someone in is a leader's decision, not an apprentice's. Do you understand?"

"Yes, Viper Strike," Pearl muttered.

"Speak up!"

"Yes, Viper Strike!"

"Good. Because of these things, you will be in charge of disposing of the Rebel's trash for the next week. No one can help you. You deserve more but we need everyone for work. Now get to your punishment, before we start out again."

"Yes, Viper Strike."

Pearl dragged her feet towards the trash pile. Her cats saw her leave Viper Strike and ran over to her, comforting her, while Pearl lugged a load of trash into the forest to bury.

"I thought I was doing well," she cried. "I am leading the Rebels to a new base, something even the warriors can't do! I was special! But now here I am, lugging trash, getting punished. Asher is the one who gets in trouble, not me!"

Moonlight meowed comfortingly.

"Thanks Moonlight. You are more than a wild cat, no matter what Viper Strike says. And you would definitely know a trap when you see one. You're smarter than a rabbit."

Just then, Sundance came running back, proudly displaying a dead rabbit in her mouth.

"You hunt rabbits!" Pearl said with a laugh. "You guys always cheer me up."

Finished with burying the trash, Pearl and her lynxes went back to the Rebels, Pearl scratching her cats in their favourite places.

Chapter 10

"What do you have here?" Viper Strike asked, as Pearl came into camp, Sundance's rabbit in her hands.

"A rabbit that Sundance caught." Pearl wanted to add a nasty retort, but knew better than to insult her leader. Even though her cats had cheered her up, she still wasn't happy with her punishment.

"Go take it to Goat Jump. He'll be able to cook something up with it." Viper Strike ordered.

"Yes, Viper Strike."

Obeying Viper Strike, Pearl went over to Goat Jump and presented the rabbit.

"Can you cook it?" she asked.

"Of course! Just give me half an hour and I'll give you a feast!" Goat Jump responded.

"Okay! I'm looking forward to it!"

Pearl left Goat Jump, and started over to Magic Healer, keeping her promise to Mary, but then Viper Strike stopped her.

"I haven't forgotten your punishment Pearl. Clear the heap, then you can visit."

Pearl sighed, and changed her course to the trash heap. Sensing her annoyance, Sundance and Moonlight snarled. Talon Claw heard them.

"I told you these beasts were wild! Snarling at us! Next thing they'll eat us in our sleep! Youngsters can never tell danger when they see it."

"Sundance and Moonlight would never hurt anyone!" Pearl protested

But the damage was done.

"They look ready to attack!" Goat Jump worried.

"They'll eat us!" Vine Hang said.

"But I've had them since they were kits! They would never do that!" Pearl protested.

"You never know. Wild cats don't change their ways," Hawk Wing said grimly.

"Yah. Some of their wildness might have stayed," Goat Jump agreed.

"My cats-" Pearl started.

"Are beasts that could kill us!" Vine Hang interrupted.

"Enough!" Viper Strike yelled, and the clearing fell silent.

* * *

They had gathered around Viper Strike, and were now waiting for her to speak. Then, she started.

"I see and understand all of your displeasure at having wild cats in our midst," Viper Strike began. "And I too share your unnerve at their seeming unpredictability."

Viper Strike was using lots of fancy words. Pearl wasn't sure if that was good or bad.

"However," Viper Strike continued, "if they are truly loyal to Pearl and will do as she commands, they would be a great asset to the Rebels. Therefore, my senior warriors and I will decide how to determine these cats' loyalties. I wish for no one to disturb these cats or I until the decision is made. Now, return to your duties."

The Rebels dispersed, slowly going back to their duties. No one openly threatened Pearl's cats, though she suspected some of the Rebels were keeping a close eye on them.

Pearl hadn't forgotten Viper Strike's order to bury the trash, and she doubted Viper Strike had either, so she started a load. After finishing, she petted her cats.

"I can't believe they don't trust you," Pearl said. "You're loyal to the Rebels and me through and through."

The two Eurasian lynxes meowed their agreement.

"I'm scared. What will they make us do?"

Sundance cocked her head, a contented look in her eyes. Pearl realized that Sundance was just living in the moment, enjoying being with Pearl and Moonlight.

"Maybe I should do that too. Come on, I have to clear the heap, and Viper Strike won't be happy if I don't finish."

* * *

After a long afternoon of hauling and burying garbage, the senior warriors and Viper Strike had still not decided what would happen with Pearl's cats, so Pearl headed over to Magic Healer, Mary, and Wolf Eye.

"Pearl! You're back!" Mary exclaimed.

Pearl laughed. "I sure am."

Magic Healer gave Pearl a warm smile. "Welcome Pearl."

"Thanks Magic Healer," Pearl responded.

"What is going to happen to your cats?" Mary asked, worried. "Surely the warriors can see that they are nice. Look at them!" Sundance and Moonlight were lying contentedly by Pearl, who was stroking them gently, and were letting out a soft, quiet purr.

"Remember we are in a time of war, where distrust and suspicion can save someone's life," Magic Healer reminded them.

"But it can also make them lose it," Pearl responded.

Just then, Wolf Eye woke up, and they rushed over to him.

"Wolf Eye!" Pearl exclaimed delightedly.

"Shh. Wolf Eye needs something to eat first, then you can talk," Magic Healer warned.

"I'm fine," Wolf Eye laughed. "You worry too much." Turning to Pearl, he asked, "So you're leading the Rebels now, are you?"

"Yah, to the place where we found. But Wolf Eye! The warriors want to kill Sundance and Moonlight!"

"Who? Sunlight and Moondance?" Wolf Eye asked, confused.

"Sundance and Moonlight! That's what I named my cats. The warriors want to kill them!" Pearl said.

"Now, now, Pearl. Surely it isn't that bad," Wolf Eye comforted her.

"I'm afraid it is," Magic Healer said. "Viper Strike said that she also doesn't like them around, and she's our leader."

"Have they decided what they are going to do about the cats?" Wolf Eye asked.

"No," Pearl responded sadly. "I hope whatever happens won't be too bad."

"Yah," Mary agreed. "I like those kitties."

Just then, Viper Strike called to the Rebels. "Let the Rebels gather!"

"I think they have decided," Magic Healer said.

"Let's hope it will be good," Pearl responded. "Come on, my cats."

Chapter 11

"Rebels," Viper Strike began, "I have recognized your distress, and, as your leader, will vanquish it from your minds. May the cats come forth."

Pearl whispered to her cats, and they stepped forward, Pearl close behind.

"The apprentice Pearl claims she can command these cats. If so, then it would be great for the Rebel's war force. If that is false, then great casualties could fall onto the Rebels. Therefore, to determine these cats' loyalties, my senior warriors and I have decided-"

Pearl could feel her heart thumping with fear.

"That they must complete three tasks, commanded by Pearl. If they succeed in all three tasks, then they live and become a trusted part of the Rebels, and Pearl earns her warrior name. If they fail in even one of the tasks, death will be the cats' by the sword."

Pearl was shocked. Her cats could be killed! She had never thought Viper Strike could be so merciless. Pearl desperately hoped that tasks wouldn't be impossible.

"The first of the three tasks will be the easiest, though it will certainly not be easy."

Pearl's hopes sank. If the first task wasn't going to be easy, and it was the easiest...

"In this task, both cats must each take a bag of pearls from the Nazi treasury."

But that was impossible! Pearl silently protested. It was guarded so well!

"In the second task, the cats must take over the outpost Wolf Eye has alerted me of."

Pearl was surprised. She hadn't realized there was an outpost near where she and Wolf Eye had done their scouting mission. Pearl figured Wolf Eye had noticed but didn't tell her so she wouldn't get scared.

"To take over the outpost, each cat must kill or scare away 10 Nazi guards. If one cat completes this task, and the other doesn't, that cat who completed the mission can move on to the final task without the failing cat."

Pearl was relieved, but also scared. If one of her cats failed the second task, then at least one lynx wouldn't drag down the other. But at the same time, she didn't want to lose either of her cats.

"For the third and final task, the cats, if both passed the second task, must work together to steal a file from the main Nazi files. This task is by far the hardest, and will be even harder if only one cat succeeds in the second task."

Steal a file! But that was impossible! Pearl didn't know what Viper Strike was thinking. Did she just not want Pearl's lynxes to have any chance of beating the tasks? But if Viper Strike didn't want the cats, she could've just said that outright. Pearl was confused.

"We will have no delay in starting these tasks," Viper Strike continued. "So the first task will take place at sunrise in two days. In those two days Pearl is excused from apprentice duties to plan.

This task must be completed in one day, from sunrise to sunset. Now, return to your duties."

Pearl stood unmoving as the rest of the Rebels went back to their duties, unsure of what to do. The tasks were impossible, but she couldn't give up hope! But even if she didn't, then how would she complete the tasks? Her mind was going in this endless loop when someone approached her from behind.

"Do you want some help?"

Pearl whirled around. Jewel Crafter was standing there, a kind but worried look on her face.

"Yes please!' Pearl agreed.

Jewel Crafter smiled. "Glad you will accept my help. I never stole any pearls myself, but I know some tactics that Pearl Snatcher taught me." Jewel Crafter's voice caught at Pearl Snatcher's name.

Pearl, waiting for Jewel Crafter to go on, thought about Pearl Snatcher. He had come to the Rebels with Jewel Crafter. They had been married, and had planned on having kids after Jewel Crafter had an apprentice that could take over her work for a while. Sadly, Pearl Snatcher died in battle along with Bear Strength, Apprentice Finder, and many others. The Rebels didn't talk about it much. The past was too hard to bear.

Jewel Crafter started up again. “Pearl Snatcher showed me some tactics, like I told you, so I can outline the basic plan. We would have to make adaptations for your cats though, since they can't crack locks or take on disguises.”

“This sounds great!” Pearl exclaimed. “Before I didn't have any idea of what to do, so anything would be better than nothing, and this is more than I could have ever expected!”

“Glad to help. Now come on, we can't waste any time.”

They planned until dark, while Sundance and Moonlight hunted for their dinner.

“Come on Pearl, let's get some dinner. We can’t do anything in the dark.” Jewel Crafter said.

“But I don't want to waste a single second!” Pearl protested.

"We can't plan in the dark, besides, I'm hungry and tired, and I bet you are too. Come on."

"Fine."

They headed back to camp, and ate some food Magic Healer had saved for them. They were almost ready for bed.

"Jewel Crafter?" Pearl asked.

"Yes?"

"Thank you."

Chapter 12

The next two days were spent in frantic planning. Over and over, Jewel Crafter and Pearl went over their plan, examining and reexamining it, looking for any possible flaws.

Pearl told her cats over and over what they were to do, desperately hoping they would understand such a complicated plan.

The cats were to run as fast as they could to the treasury that was a couple hour's walk from the Rebel's resting stop. They had stayed in the clearing to give time for Pearl to plan.

After getting to the treasury, the cats were to watch the door, and while it was open, slip inside, one at a time if need be. Then they would sniff around, and find the scent of pearls, then follow that scent to the vault. Then, they would wait for someone to open the vault, slip inside, and wait for the people to exit the vault. Then, when it was safe to move around, the Eurasian lynxes would pick the lightest bags, then wait for the vault door to open. After it opens, they would slip outside into the main treasury, wait and slip outside of the treasury, and run back to the Rebels as fast as they could. The plan seemed so straightforward and simple, but Pearl knew so many things could go wrong, no matter how much she and Jewel Crafter reviewed their plan. All she could do was hope that all would be in their favor.

Then, Viper Strike called out. “Let the Rebels gather!”

It was time.

After the Rebels had come together, Viper Strike began. “The two days designated for preparation for the first task had ended. I hope Pearl has a set plan in place. The rules are as follows: both cats must each bring back one bag of pearls, and must return by sundown. No one may help them, except Pearl when she commands the cats. Now, let the task begin!”

Quickly, Pearl went over the instructions one last time with Sundance and Moonlight. Then at the end, she said

"Go! As fast as you can!" and the cats were off.

"And they're off!" Asher yelled.

"Asher," Hawk Wing warned.

"What?"

"Now is not the time for your jokes."

"Fine."

But Asher was right. The cats were off, off on a mission that seemed impossible, but had to be completed for the lynxes to keep their lives.

Chapter 13

"Pack up camp!" Viper Strike called.

Everybody was moving. Pearl figured they had but a day's march to the new base. Viper Strike had said if her cats were truly loyal to her they would be able to track her to the new base. Pearl hoped she was right.

"Which direction Pearl?" Viper Strike asked.

With a quick check at their surroundings, Pearl knew. "This way! Follow me!"

* * *

Pearl stopped the Rebels as they came to the clearing with the tree. It had been a long journey, and the apprentices flopped down to rest, but the warriors weren't ready to do that yet.

"Where's the new base?" Hawk Wing asked. "I don't see anything."

"Yah," Goat Jump agreed. "The only thing here is that tree."

"The tree is the base!" Pearl exclaimed.

"But how?" Vine Hang asked.

Pearl scrambled up into the tree. "There's a hole in here!" momentarily forgetting her worries about their tasks, Pearl excitedly told the warriors about the new base. "There's a hole that leads down to easily dug soil! Probably in a few months we could dig it out and create an underground bunker!"

"What if it caves in?" Goat Jump worried.

"We can use logs to strengthen the ceiling and walls," Vine Hang said.

Viper Strike nodded. "Good." Then, raising her voice she called, "Let the Rebels gather!"

The Rebels gathered around Viper Strike. After everyone was there, Viper Strike began. "This is as good of a base as we could have hoped for, given the circumstances. Thank you Pearl, Wolf Eye.

Also, Pearl and Wolf Eye, did you find any springs or streams from which we can get water?"

"Yes," Pearl said. "I don't know how to direct anyone to it, but I can find it."

"Good. You will lead a water patrol. Hawk Wing, will you organize food, building, and water patrols for the next little while?" Viper Strike asked.

"Of course," Hawk Wing agreed.

"Good." Viper Strike said. "Everyone go to Hawk Wing to see what you are to do. Goat Jump, Lucas and I will guard. Now, return to your duties."

After Viper Strike dismissed them, Pearl strode over to Hawk Wing to see who would be in her water patrol.

"Good, there you are, Pearl," Hawk Wing said. "You will lead Jewel Crafter, and Mike. Look for litter along the way that can be used for water storage. The Nazis are sure to have lefts something."

Pearl and the rest of her group found each other while Hawk Wing organized more patrols.

"I will lead Vine Hang and Lily." Hawk Wing said. "We will be on food patrol. Mary, you're helping Magic Healer. Talon Claw, you are on building duty. Haul logs to the tree, dig out the underground, whatever you can do."

"Why am I, all alone, doing the hardest task?" Talon Claw grumbled. "You people are getting lazy, putting the hard stuff on the shoulders of your elders."

"Talon Claw," Hawk Wing rebuked. "You know we can only spare only one warrior right now for building, and it's just luck of the draw you got the job."

"Not luck of the draw if you chose!"

Pearl and her patrol headed out then, and they didn't hear the rest of the argument. They went along slowly, looking carefully for garbage to hold water in and stopping to pick it up when they found some. Finally, they could hear the stream.

"We're here!" Mike announced.

"We know that Mike." Pearl said. "But be quiet. The Nazis may have set up an outpost near here since Wolf Eye and I were here."

"Pearl's right," Jewel Crafter agreed. "Stay down low and be as quiet as a mouse."

The group crept along in complete silence, since all of them had mastered the skills of hiding their trails and stalking. After a bit, Mike whispered, “I think it’s clear.” “Good,” Pearl whispered back. “Let's go and fill up our containers, but be very quiet.”

“Got it, Sergeant!" Mike quietly joked, and they crept out to the steam, quickly filled their containers, then left.

Traveling back through the forest, they had to be very careful not to spill their water, walking around fallen trees instead of jumping over, and just going through the clear parts of the forest. It was tedious work, and even though they were very careful, at least a liter of water must have been spilled on that journey. The slow progress gave Pearl plenty of time to worry and worry about the tasks, and soon her mind was lost in an endless maze of worries.

Then, Jewel Crafter spoke, startling her from her trance as they neared the camp. “We need a better way to get water.”

"Yah," Mike agreed. "We were so slow, Hawk Wing's group made it back before us!"

"Ah, well. They probably didn't have to go as far," Pearl reasoned.

"Or be as careful," Jewel Crafter added.

"Come on, let's go drop the water off," Mike said.

After dropping off the water, Pearl said a quick hello to the other apprentices and then went to the trash heap to fulfill more of her punishment.

Finishing that, she went over to where Magic Healer, Mary and Wolf Eye were.

"Hi guys!" she called.

"Hi Pearl!" They greeted her.

Pearl settled down beside them.

"Do you think the kitties will pass the first task?" Mary asked.

"I hope so," Pearl said. "I couldn't live without them."

"I'm sure they will," Wolf Eye comforted them. "They've been devoted to Pearl since the moment we found them in the forest. It seems so long ago."

"It was!" Pearl agreed. "They're full grown now!"

"I'm sure the cats will be fine," Magic Healer agreed. "They would do anything in the world for you, Pearl, even if it kills them."

Pearl smiled. "Maybe."

Magic Healer laughed. "I'm sure of it. Now, I have some good news. Wolf Eye is fit enough to return to warrior duties. I would have told you earlier, Wolf Eye, but I thought Pearl would like to hear it with you."

"Yay!" Pearl exclaimed. She twirled around and hugged Wolf Eye. "I've missed you during warrior duties."

Wolf Eye smiled, and patted Pearl on the back. "And so have I. Now come on, I want something to eat."

* * *

Dinner was finished, and most of the Rebels were lounging around, enjoying a bit of rest with nothing to do, but not Pearl. The deadline for the first task was drawing nearer and nearer, and as her worry rose she began pacing back and forth. Where were Sundance and Moonlight? If they didn't come soon, they would fail the first task, and they would be killed! Pearl worried on and on as the sun sank lower and lower in the sky.

Chapter 14

The dark was almost there, but the two lynxes weren't. Pearl had taken to running around the trees near the new base, desperately trying to catch a glimpse of a shadow that could be her cats. Glancing up, Pearl saw that there must only a minute left till the deadline. Where were her cats? Then, she saw two shadows flickering through the trees. Could it be? Or was her desperate mind playing tricks on her?

Pearl started closer to the two shadows, not moving her eyes off them in case they disappeared. The shadows were coming closer. Were they her cats?

"Meow!"

They were!

"Sundance! Moonlight!" Pearl called with delight. She ran as fast as her legs could carry her, and then swept her cats into her arms. Looking loser, she saw both cats each had a bag of pearls in their mouths. “You really did it!” she exclaimed. The lynxes purred happily.

Just then, Viper Strike noticed the cat’s arrival. “Let the Rebels gather!”

Full of happiness, Pearl went over to Viper Strike with the rest of the Rebels.

“Pearl and her cats have completed their first mission,” Viper Strike announced. “Well done.”

Some grumbling arose at this, but none of it was loud enough to be heard. After waiting for it to be finished, Viper Strike continued. “Bring the pearls forth.”

Pearl whispered to her cats, and the lynxes stepped forward, dropped the pearls at Viper Strike’s feet, and stepped back. Leaning down, Viper Strike took the pearls into her hands. “Good. Each cat has brought back a bag of pearls, succeeding in the first task. Jewel Crafter, come and take these pearls.”

Jewel Crafter stepped forward, took the pearls, nodded to Pearl, her cats, and Viper Strike, then stepped back.

“Now the cats have completed the first mission,” Viper Strike continued, “they will move on to the second task. In the next task, each cat must kill or scare away ten of the Nazis that are guarding the nearby outpost, in order for the Rebels to loot it. As before, Pearl has two days to plan, and in those two days she is excused from warrior duties. As in the first task, the cats will have one day to complete the second task. Goat Jump and I will observe the cats and take a tally of how many guards they have disposed of. Now, return to your duties."

Pearl led her cats over to Wolf Eye. "Wolf Eye?" she asked.

"Yes, Pearl?' he answered.

"Can you help me with the second task?"

"Of course!"

"Can we start now?"

"No, it's too dark. We can start in the morning, though."

"Fine."

*   *   *

Tired, Pearl got into her makeshift bed, her cats snuggled in around her. Fatigue weighed down her eyelids, but her racing thoughts allowed her no rest. Would her cats complete the second task? Would the guards of the outpost overwhelm them? What would happen if one cat took down eleven guards, and one took down nine? Could the guards call reinforcements? If so, would the cats have to fight those Nazis too? Or would Viper Strike and Goat Jump help them? What if the reinforcements came, overwhelmed her cats, and the warriors deserted them? All of these worries and more flooded over her as she drifted off to sleep.

*　　　*　　　*

The next day, Wolf Eye and Pearl spent the whole morning planning, then went to get a quick lunch at noon.

"Wolf Eye," Vine Hang said, approaching them, "Hawk Wing says you're on my food patrol this afternoon."

""I don't know if I can, I'm helping Pearl plan for the next task," Wolf Eye responded.

"That was an order, not a question," said Hawk Wing, coming up behind them. "We need all hands on deck."

"Oh, alright," Wolf Eye sighed. "I'll be there after lunch." he turned to Pearl, as Vine Hang and Hawk Wing walked away. "I'm sorry Pearl, but I can't go against orders. Maybe Jewel Crafter can help you again?"

"I'll see," said Pearl glumly. After finishing her lunch, she walked to Jewel Crafter, the lynxes trailing behind her.

"Jewel Crafter?" she asked.

"Yes, Pearl?" responded Jewel Crafter.

"Will you help me with the second task? Wolf Eye is on patrol."

"I'm afraid I can't. I have to make weapons out of the pearls your cats got."

"Oh, well, thanks anyways."

"I'm really sorry I can't help, but good luck!"

"Thanks."

Worried, Pearl walked away, her shoulders sagging with despair. Who could help her? She couldn't make a plan alone! Then she heard someone behind her.

“I can help you Pearl.”

Pearl turned around to see Mike behind her.

“Goat Jump taught me some tactics that might be useful,” Mike said. “I saw Wolf Eye and Jewel Crafter couldn’t help you, so I just thought I'd ask. If you don't want help, its fine, I won't be upset…”

“No, it’s great! I would love your help!” Pearl exclaimed happily. “Thank you so, so, much!”

Delighted, Pearl and Mike started planning. They worked till dark, only stopping for a brief dinner. After finishing the plan started by Pearl and Wolf Eye, they then ironed out the kinks and possible mishaps, reshaping the plan along the way. Then, after the last rays of sunlight were gone, they settled into bed. Pearl had no trouble getting to sleep that night, the planning had exhausted her.

*   *   *

In the morning, Mike had no immediate duties, so they had another morning of successful planning. Then, they stopped for a quick lunch break.

After a bit, Goat Jump came over to them. “Mike,” he said, “we need to do some training. Meet me at the base of the tree when you are done with lunch.” with that, he strode away.

Mike turned to Pearl. “I’m really sorry,” he said. “But I can't go against Goat Jump’s orders.”

“It’s alright,” Pearl said. “You’ve helped me a lot. Maybe Jewel Crafter or Wolf Eye will be free again.”

“I hope so,” Mike said. Just then, he finished his lunch. “See you, and good luck!”

“Thanks! Bye!”

Pearl ran over to Wolf Eye, and asked him if he could plan with her.

“Of course,” Wolf Eye said. “If nothing comes up.”

They planned until dark, finding the kinks in the plan that Pearl and Mike hadn’t. After dark and dinner, Pearl whispered the plan over and over to her cats, getting it stuck in her head, and hopefully her cats’ too, before she allowed herself to rest.

They were to sneak up on the Nazi outpost and wait for the guards to come out. Viper Strike and Goat Jump would each watch one of the lynxes to see how many guards they either killed or scared away. After the first guards came out, the cats would have to frighten them enough so that the other guards would come out, but not enough to call reinforcements. That was the risky part. The rest was easy. Once the soldiers came out, the cats would kill or scare them away, until the outpost was unguarded. If they did this before dark, then they would succeed in the second task. Then, Viper Strike, Goat Jump, and the cats would go back to camp.

*　　　*　　　*

In the morning, at dawn, Viper Strike called the Rebels. “Let the Rebels gather!”

“Can you wait a little longer,” Talon Claw grumbled. “I don't know about you people, but I value my sleep.”

“Then it wouldn't be fair to the cats,” Wolf Eye reminded him. “They need the full day to complete the task.”

Then, Viper Strike began. “It is time for Pearl’s cats to complete the second task. The rules are simple, they must each either kill or scare away ten Nazis soldiers by sunset. Goat Jump and I will each be watching one of the cats to see how many guards they dispose of. Because this is an individual task, if one of the cats completes the task and the other does not, then the succeeding cat can move on to the third task without the other cat. Hawk Wing, you will be in charge in my stead. Now, let the task begin!”

The cats raced off, heading into the forest, Viper Strike and Goat Jump running behind. Pearl desperately hoped both of her cats would complete the second task, but she had a fearful sense that one might not…

Chapter 15

"Pearl, you're on the food patrol with Vine Hang, Lucas, and Wolf Eye. Wolf Eye is leading." Hawk Wing was organizing the day's patrols. "I will help Talon Claw with building. Mary, you're with Magic Healer. The rest of you are on water patrol. Jewel Crafter leads."

Just as Pearl was leaving with the water patrol, Magic Healer came up to Hawk Wing. "Hawk Wing, can the patrols look for herbs?" she asked. We're getting low on them."

"Of course." Hawk Wing turned to the patrols. "Look for healing herbs."

Wolf Eye nodded, and the patrol set off.

*   *   *

"Pearl, Lucas, look on the ground for berries and fallen nuts," Wolf Eye ordered. "Vine Hang and I will look in the trees."

"Got it," they said.

The patrol scavenged all morning and stopped for lunch. Just as they were finishing up, they heard a rustle.

"Get down!" Wolf Eye whispered. They ducked down, quickly hiding all signs of their presence.

"Those Rebels must be close," a gruff voice said. "Those lynxes wouldn't be so persistent without someone egging them on."

Pearl saw through the covering of her hiding spot two soldiers with the Nazi symbol on their clothes.

"Yah. I heard that some of the guards have fled," the second soldier answered. Then, the soldiers walked away. After waiting a few moments to make sure the Nazi soldiers were really gone, the food patrol crept out from their hiding places.

"That was close," Lucas whispered, still afraid of being heard.

"Yah," Pearl agreed, matching his whisper.

"It's disturbing that they know we are here," Vine Hang said in a regular voice.

"Maybe we shouldn't have attacked the outpost."

"Maybe," said Wolf Eye in a voice that sounded like he did not agree. "But Viper Strike needs to know about this. Come on, let's get back to camp."

Shaken by what they had heard, the food patrol went back to camp, bringing along the food they had found in the morning. After they had gotten back, Wolf Eye went to Hawk Wing to give a report. "Hawk Wing," he began, "we saw two Nazi soldiers about 30 km from this camp. They passed by without knowledge of our presence, but what we heard led me to believe that they know we are here. We should be very careful."

"I will inform Viper Strike," Hawk Wing said. "Now, go drop off your food and come help Talon Claw and me."

The food patrol set their day's finding with the few other fruits, nuts and berries, then went to join Talon Claw and Hawk Wing. After the food patrol joined them, Hawk Wing assigned them their tasks. "Vine Hang, Wolf Eye and Pearl, you are digging. Lucas, you are with me and Talon Claw. We are hauling logs."

Pearl sent Lucas a sorry shrug. With Talon Claw around, he wasn't going to have much fun. "See you!" she called.

Pearl went to the digging. It was hard work, but did not require much concentration, and her mind began to wander to the tasks. Would her cats succeed? Would only one of them? Would neither of them? What about the third task? It was impossible to break into the Nazi file room! People planned for years, and those plans still failed sometimes. Pearl was sure she wouldn't even have a half a year to plan. How would she do it? Were her cats destined to be killed, trying to break in? Maybe they were.

* * *

After a couple of hours, there was a fairly good sized hole, Pearl's back was aching from the effort, and the water patrol was finally back. There was no sign of

Viper Strike, Goat Jump, or the lynxes though. Where were they?

"Dinner!" Vine Hang called. He had been excused halfway through the digging to prepare it. Pearl sighed with the relief that she could stop digging, and got up for dinner, wondering what sorry excuse for a meal Vine Hang had cooked up.

* * *

Pearl didn't eat well, she was so worried. Well, nobody ate much of Vine Hang's gross mush, with who knows what ingredients, but even for that, Pearl did not eat much. What was happening with her cats? Would they complete the second task? Would they fail? Then, through her worrying, Pearl heard a voice.

"We're back!"

Pearl twirled around to see her leader, her cats, and Goat Jump emerge through the trees.

* * *

"Let the Rebels gather!" Viper Strike called, and the Rebels, eager to hear the verdict on the cats, crowded around her. Pearl's lynx followed Pearl into the mass.

"The cats have finished the second task," Viper Strike began, "and I will announce if they have succeeded or failed later. For now, Goat Jump and I need dinner. Return to your duties."

Pearl was worried. She wondered if Viper Strike didn't want to announce bad news, afraid to break Pearl's heart. And the tone in which she said 'succeeded or failed', suggested that at least one of the cats had failed. Maybe she was just being a worry wart, but Pearl was sure something was up.

"Come on Pearl," Wolf Eye called. "Come train. It will take your mind off the tasks."

"Okay, Wolf Eye," Pearl agreed worriedly. She was sure she wouldn't be able to focus on the training. But she followed Wolf Eye, while her lynxes ran off to hunt.

They had practiced for an hour, Pearl quickly picking up a complicated sword technique.

"Soon I will have nothing to teach you," Wolf Eye commented as they headed back to camp. "Viper Strike will soon have to start thinking about your warrior name."

"I can't wait!" Pearl exclaimed, for a minute forgetting about the tasks in the exciting prospect of her warrior name. "I wonder what my warrior name will be. Will you have a say in it?"

"I will tell Viper Strike your strengths and weaknesses, but besides that, Viper Strike will decide."

Then, they were at the camp, and Viper Strike was striding to the center of it. "Let the Rebels gather!" she called.

"It's time," Pearl said under her breath, as her cats ran over to join her. "Will my cats live or die?"

Chapter 16

"I am now fed and rested," Viper Strike began, "and am ready to tell you the fates of these cats, whether they succeeded or failed, whether they will live or die."

Pearl didn't like that. The way Viper Strike stretched it out, prolonged the time till she would announce the cats' fates, made Pearl wonder if she was avoiding a hard task. It could just be Viper Strike using fancy talk, but Pearl wasn't so sure.

"In the second task," Viper Strike continued, "these two cats had to each kill or scare away ten Nazi guards, in order for the Rebels to plunder the outpost, without any warriors getting hurt in the process. The task was to be completed by sundown. And remember, if one cat fails and the other cat succeeds, then the succeeding cat may go on without the failing cat."

Pearl didn't like how Viper Strike said the last part. It was like she was preparing them for something, something that was not good.

"The first cat, named Sundance," Viper Strike continued. "Killed one Nazi soldier…"

Pearl held her breath.

"And scared away nine others, completing the second task."

Pearl breathed a sigh of relief. At least Sundance was okay. Beside her, Sundance purred, as if understanding that her life was safe. Pearl hoped with all her heart that Moonlight's was too.

"The second cat, named Moonlight," Viper Strike said, "killed two Nazi soldiers…"

Pearl sought out Wolf Eye's hand and squeezed it hard, anxious.

"And scared away eight others, completing the second task."

Pearl could have jumped for joy. Both of her cats were safe! Instead, she opted for hugging her cats.

"Both cats have successfully completed the second task," Viper Strike continued, "letting the Rebels access much needed supplies. But the final task is still to come. This task will be the hardest one. In the third task the cats must sneak in to the Nazi file room and steal a file. That file will be examined for possible weaknesses in the Nazi empire. Because of the enormity of this task, Pearl will have three days to plan, and the cats will have a week to carry it out, from sunrise on the first day till sunset on the seventh. In the three days of planning, Pearl is dismissed from warrior duties. Now, return to your duties."

Pearl didn't know what to think. Three days of planning? But other people had spent years planning for a mission like her's and still failed! What was she to do? Was Viper Strike setting them up for failure on purpose? If so, why? She could've just sentenced the cats to death, and that would be that. Or maybe she wanted it to be more subdued, because some of the Rebels liked the cats? Whatever the reason, Pearl wasn't going to let it take her cats away. She set her shoulders, and decided that her cats would not fail. They could not. Pearl wouldn't let them. Then, she turned to her friends for help on how to complete an uncompletable task.

*   *   *

"Let the Rebels gather!" Viper Strike called.

The three days of planning were over. Pearl had a set plan in place, although she wasn't at all certain it would work. So much of it was up to chance. It was kind of like how the lynxes stole the pearls, but more complex, and infinitely more dangerous.

The cats were to travel to the Nazi capital as swiftly as they could, following Nazi paths and roads while keeping to the undergrowth. Wolf Eye estimated that it was two day's run from the new camp to the capital, four days there and back, so that left three days to carry out the file stealing. It wasn't a lot, but Pearl hoped it would be enough. To steal the file, the cats would sneak around until they found evidence of the file room, hopefully on the first day there, and creep inside the building, just like when they stole the pearls. Watch, slip in, hide. Watch, slip in, hide. Watch, slip in, hide…, until they get into the file room. They would choose a file at random, then repeat the process all over again. Watch, slip out, hide…. After they got out, they would run back to the Rebels as fast as they could, and hopefully make the deadline. Hopefully.

Then, Viper Strike started speaking, and Pearl turned away from her thoughts.

"It is time for the third and final task," Viper Strike began, "in this task, these two cats must steal a file from under the nose of Adolf Hitler himself."

Pearl gulped. When Viper Strike phrased it like that, the odds of her cats succeeding didn't look too good.

"They will have until sundown in seven days' time. If they are caught, then they fail. Now, let the task begin!"

Pearl watched as Sundance and Moonlight raced off into the sunrise, to their probable doom. She was already starting to worry about them. It would be a hard week.

Chapter 17

The next day, Pearl went over to Mary for a chat in one of her infrequent breaks.

"Hi Mary!" she called.

"Hi!" Mary returned.

"What have you been doing?" Pearl asked.

"Helping Magic Healer. She says I'm really good at identifying herbs!"

"That's great! Maybe Viper Strike will apprentice you to her!"

"Hope so!"

Just then Hawk Wing called Pearl. "Pearl! You're on water patrol!"

"One second!" she called back, then turned to Mary. "See you soon?"

"See you soon," Mary agreed.

Pearl walked over to Hawk Wing.

"You're on patrol getting supplies from the outpost, with Viper Strike, Wolf Eye, Jewel Crafter and Lily. Viper Strike leads," he said.

“Okay,” responded Pearl. She walked over to her patrol.

“Let’s go,” Viper Strike ordered, seeing Pearl joining them.

And so they left.

✳ ✳ ✳

After a morning getting to the outpost, they collected the supplies without trouble and were making good progress back. They were over half way to the camp when they spotted Magic Healer and Mary, and went over to them.

Hi!” said Pearl, Mary, and Lily at the same time. Then they giggled.

“What are you two doing?” Wolf Eye asked.

“Collecting herbs,” Magic Healer responded.

“Is Mary here to carry them back?” asked Viper Strike.

“Yes, but she is helping me collect them too. She’s getting really good at identifying healing herbs.” Magic Healer said.

"That's good. You need an apprentice." Viper Strike commented.

"Do you think I could?" Mary asked, jumping into the conversation.

"Maybe," Viper Strike said. "Maybe."

"It would be awesome!' Mary exclaimed.

"I'm not yet sure, so don't get your hopes up," Viper Strike warned.

"I won't," Mary said, trying to control the eager look on her face.

"We should get going," said Wolf Eye, looking at the sky. "If we don't start soon, then it will be dark before we get back."

After saying goodbye to Mary and Magic Healer, they headed back to camp.

*　　*　　*

"You're finally back!" Asher exclaimed, as the patrol entered the camp.

"Asher," Hawk Wing warned. "Don't be rude."

"I wasn't rude," Asher protested. "Right?" He looked to the water patrol. "Right?"

Pearl laughed. "Sure."

*   *   *

After eating a quick but delicious supper, since Goat Jump was back, and Vine Hang didn't have to take over for him, Pearl talked with her friends, then went to bed, ready for a tough day of work.

*   *   *

The next morning, just after Pearl had eaten breakfast, Viper Strike called the Rebels. "Let the Rebels gather!"

The Rebels gathered around her. Pearl wondered why Viper Strike had called a meeting. As far as she knew, there were no threats to the Rebels, or things to be done, besides the tasks, but there was nothing to be done for them. How Pearl hoped that her cats would be alright. Pearl tore herself away from her worrying. Viper

Strike must have wanted to check in with the Rebels for some reason, but she could've just asked them individually. Unless… one of the apprentices was done their training! Lily had been a part of the Rebels the longest, so it was probably her. Excited by her revelation, Pearl impatiently waited for Viper Strike to begin.

"There is one of the apprentices here that have completed their training," Viper Strike started.

Pearl smiled. She was right! A warrior ceremony!

"Thanks to their mentor," Viper Strike continued, "they have learned the arts of combat, survival, and the skill of their mentor. In this training, they have developed their own skill that has been seen and acknowledged, and they will get their warrior name based on that skill. Today, this apprentice will be made into a warrior, as they deserve. Lily, come forward."

Pearl was right! It was Lily's warrior ceremony. She eagerly watched Lily walk towards Viper Strike.

"Lily," said Viper Strike, "do you promise to protect the Rebels, even with your life, and put the Rebels above everything, using the skills you have been taught?"

Lily shivered with excitement. "I do."

"Then, by these words," Viper Strike said, "I give you your warrior name. Lily, from this moment onward, you will be known as Pearl Wielder, after your skill of crafting pearls."

"Pearl Wielder! Pearl Wielder!" the Rebels chanted.

Pearl rushed forward to congratulate her friend.

Chapter 18

Pearl was on building patrol with Wolf Eye, Goat Jump, Mike and Pearl Wielder, the afternoon after Pearl Wielder's warrior ceremony. Magic Healer had gone out of the camp, but left Mary behind so that she could sort herbs.

The digging was going very well. They already had hollowed out the hole into a cave at the bottom, and the cave could fit two warriors comfortably. The entrance had been hidden so well even Pearl had a hard time finding it, and she was the one who discovered it. Digging the base was hard work, but it would be impossible to find if you didn't know where to look.

Then, Asher came running into the camp. "Help! Help! Lucas sprained his ankle and he's hurt really badly!"

The camp erupted into chaos, everyone talking over each other.

"Is he alright?"

"Can Magic Healer help?"

"How far is it?"

"Will he be alright?"

"Quiet!" Pearl yelled. "This is getting us nowhere," she continued when everyone had stopped talking. "If everyone is talking over each other, then no one will get their point across, and Lucas will still be hurt!" She turned to Asher. "How far is it?"

"About five kilometers." he responded.

"Okay." She turned to the rest of the patrol. "Did Magic Healer say where she was going?"

They shook their heads.

"Can Lucas wait?" Pearl asked Asher.

"Maybe, but I don't think so."

"Maybe Mary can help?" Mike suggested. "She has been helping out Magic Healer."

"Good idea!" Pearl praised. "I'll go get her." She ran over to Mary. "Mary, Lucas sprained his ankle, and Magic Healer is out. Can you help?"

"Of course!" Mary agreed. "Where is he?"

"Just follow Asher back."

“Okay. I'll just get some herbs.”

As soon as Mary was ready, she and Asher set off. A little while later, Magic Healer came back. “Where’s Mary?” she asked.

“Tending to Lucas. He sprained his ankle on patrol and you were out, so we sent her,” Pearl Wielder answered.

“He's in good hands,” Magic Healer responded.

* * *

Later, Viper Strike, Mary, Asher, Lucas, and Hawk Wing emerged from the trees, with Hawk Wing supporting Lucas. Viper Strike turned to Pearl. “Asher told me you called everyone who was panicking to order. Good job.”

“Thanks Viper Strike!’ Pearl said, embarrassed.

Then Viper Strike turned to Mike. “Asher told me you were the one who had the idea for sending Mary in Magic Healer’s place. Good job.”

“Thanks!” said Mike.

Finally, Viper Strike turned to Mary. "You did very well tending to Lucas, especially since you are not apprenticed to Magic Healer. Good job."

"Thank you!" Mary exclaimed.

Just then, Magic Healer came up beside Viper Strike. "Can I talk to you?" she asked. "Mary can tend to Lucas."

"Of course," Viper Strike agreed. The two walked off to have a chat in private, and Pearl went to Mary and Lucas to see how she could help.

Chapter 19

The next day, Pearl had a busy morning of a food patrol, and came back to camp just in time for lunch.

She went over to Goat Jump, and loaded up her plate. Lunch was nuts and berries. Then, she sat down with the other apprentices and Pearl Wielder.

"Better than some other days, right?" Asher asked.

"Definitely," Mike agreed. "Remember when we had pig's feet?"

"Yah," Pearl Wielder said. "I was gross."

"Good thing we can get the supplies from the outpost soon," said Lucas, who had been helped over by Vine Hang. His ankle wasn't broken, thankfully, but it would be a few weeks until he would be on his feet again. He didn't get off easy though. Magic Healer had plenty of sitting down tasks for him to do, as well as Goat Jump while he was cooking. Lucas was turning out to be a good cook, and although he said he would rather do warrior duties any day, Pearl didn't believe him.

"We can get them because of Pearl's cats!" Asher exclaimed. "Let's have a round of applause for them and Pearl!"

"Not me," Pearl protested. "My cats did all the work."

"But you planned," Lucas argued.

"With help," Pearl disagreed.

"But you did most of it," said Pearl Wielder. "Or did someone else somehow tell your two cats how to do it?"

Pearl laughed. "You got me. But please, don't do a round of applause even if it's just so we don't irritate Talon Claw."

"Alright," Asher agreed. "But only because I don't want to deal with Talon Claw."

Then, they ate in silence, gobbling down the food. When they had finished, they started talking again.

"Goat Jump said I might be a warrior soon," Mike said.

"That's great!" Asher said excitedly. "Hawk Wing thinks it will be a while until I get my warrior name. He says I have to learn my manners first."

Pearl laughed. "You do, Asher. Wolf Eye says I might get mine soon." silently, she thought, I hope my cats are there to see it.

"Cool!" said Lucas. "Vine Hang said it would be a while till I get my warrior name, but I'm the newest apprentice, so it makes sense."

Just then, Mary came over. "Can I sit here?" she asked nervously, holding her plate. Pearl figured Mary was late to lunch so she could finish up drying or sorting herbs.

"Of course!" Pearl Wielder said.

"Sit right down!' said Lucas.

Asher did a silly bow. "At your service."

"Asher," said Pearl, laughing. "Have you forgotten you're a Rebel apprentice, not a waiter?"

"Wait, I'm not a waiter?" Asher asked in mock disbelief.

Giggling, Mary sat down. "What were you guys talking about?" she asked as she daintily ate her food.

"When we might get our warrior names," Mike responded.

"I hope I will get to be Magic Healer's apprentice," Mary said dreamily.

"That would be cool," Pearl said. "Then I wouldn't be the only girl apprentice."

Then they finished up, said goodbye, and headed off in their separate ways, to go do more work.

Chapter 20

Pearl had been scattering the dug-up dirt, and it had left her dusty and tired. She went over to a cleanish puddle to clean herself off slightly, then went for dinner. Goat Jump was serving roasted nuts, berries, a squirrel that had been caught that day, and roasted cattails. Pearl loaded up her plate, then went over to where her friends were sitting.

"Guess what?" Mike asked.

"What?" said Asher.

"I caught the squirrel!" Mike said proudly.

"Cool! I can never figure out how to hit them with the arrow. They're too fast!"

"I can help you with that! You just need to calculate where the squirrel will move next."

"How?"

"I'll show you tomorrow, but for now I can give you some pointers if you want."

"Okay!"

"So first you..."

Pearl's ears drifted to another conversation.

"I hope I'll get to be Magic Healer's apprentice!" Mary said.

"I'm sure you will," comforted Pearl Wielder. "You have a knack for healing."

"You think?" Mary asked, proud.

"I know." Pearl Wielder picked up a flower from the ground. "Is this a healing herb?"

"No, I think it's poisonous."

"Good thing I didn't eat it then."

Pearl's eyes drifted over to where Lucas was hungrily wolfing down his food. "Slow down!" she laughed. "Why are you eating so fast?"

"I'm hungry," said Lucas, not looking up from his dinner.

"You should savor it. You don't have much left." Pearl said.

"Too bad. I don't fancy going back for seconds with Talon Claw around."

"I agree."

"What did you do this afternoon?"

"Building."

"Cool. I did battle training. Vine Hang says I'm really good at the battle stance."

"Wow! I have so much trouble with it."

"Well, I did something like it sometimes before I joined the Rebels, so I've had some practice."

"That's cool. If you don't mind me asking, why did you do it? I mean, I don't think there are many battles out there."

"It just sort of calms me. It sounds weird, I know, but it does."

"It's not weird. Sundance and Moonlight do that for me too. They kind of sense what I'm feeling and react to it, so they know how to calm me. And sometimes they feel the same mood as I'm feeling. That's what started the tasks. I was grumpy, so my cats reacted, and Talon Claw thought they were being dangerous."

"Wow. So they were just reacting to your mood?"

"Yah."

"How did they sense it?"

"I don't know."

"Maybe it's the first time this has ever happened."

"That would be cool."

"Also, if that is true, then you are really lucky to have them."

"Yah, even if it gets me in trouble like the tasks."

"Yah, but don't worry about that. I'm sure they will succeed."

"I hope you're right."

Chapter 21

The next day after breakfast, Pearl walked over to Mary, who was sorting herbs.

"Hi Mary!" greeted Pearl.

"Hi Pearl!" responded Mary. "What have you been up to?"

"Work. Water, food and building patrols. They never seem to end. How about you?"

"Helping Magic Healer. She let me tend to Asher when he scraped his leg. She says I'm getting really good."

"That's great! Soon you will be an apprentice with me!"

"I hope so!"

They sat in companionable silence, observing the camp.

"Pearl!" Hawk Wing called. "Come haul dirt!"

"Coming!' she hollered, and turned to Mary. "Bye."

"Bye!"

Pearl ran over to the building patrol, exchanged greetings, and set her back to the work.

*　　　*　　　*

"Let the Rebels gather!" Viper Strike called. It was just after dinner, and Pearl was glad for the extra time before bed. Wondering what the meeting was about, she joined the rest of the Rebels.

"Today it is time for the naming of a new apprentice," Viper Strike began.

Pearl beamed. It was Mary's apprentice ceremony!

"This child's name is Mary," Viper Strike continued. "Mary, come forward."

Trembling with excitement, Mary gracefully walked towards Viper Strike.

'Magic Healer," Viper Strike said, "Will you mentor Mary to the best of your abilities, teaching her in the arts of combat, survival, and your own skill?""

"I will,' Magic Healer said solemnly.

Viper Strike turned to Mary. "Mary, will you listen to your mentor, Magic Healer, and learn how to be a warrior of the Rebels?"

"I will," Mary answered excitedly.

"Then Mary, you are now an apprentice of the Rebels. Listen to your mentor, and you will learn great skills that will show us your warrior name."

The Rebels started cheering. "Mary! Mary!"

Pearl ran to Mary, wanting to be the first to congratulate her.

"`I knew you would be Magic Healer's apprentice!' she exclaimed.

"Yah," Pearl Wielder agreed. "I told you."

"Thanks!" Mary said happily. "I still can't believe it. It's a dream come true!"

"You won't be saying that when you're hauling trash," Asher joked. "Congrats, Mary."

"Thanks Asher," Mary said. "And I think Magic Healer's apprentice wouldn't have to carry trash. I'm healing the Rebels, you know!"

Mike laughed. "You'll see. No one gets out of garbage duty."

Lucas limped over, smiling. “You’re one of us now!”

“Yay!” Mary said excitedly.

“There’s another girl apprentice now!’ Pearl said. “Soon we will outnumber the boys!”

Mary laughed. “Go girls, go!”

Just then Vine Hang came up to them. “Sorry to be a party pooper,” he said, “but it’s time to sleep. To bed, all of you.”

“Fine,” they groaned.

“Night, guys!” Mary said.

“Night, new apprentice!” they called back, then they got into their beds, and everyone but Pearl drifted to sleep. Pearl stayed up, unable to sleep because of her worry about the tasks. Were her cats all right? Were they hurt? Would they fail? Finally, Pearl fell asleep, but her dreams turned into nightmares of her cats failing the tasks.

Dreams are sometimes right.

Nightmares too.

Chapter 22

As Pearl was getting up, she remembered that it was two days til the deadline of the third task. Two days! Hopefully, it was also just two days until she saw her cats. Hopefully.

After eating breakfast, Pearl went to Wolf Eye to train.

"What are we doing today?" Pearl asked him.

"Today we will work on your battle stance," Wolf Eye said. "You certainly could improve on it."

"Fine," Pearl groaned.

"Come on. Put your right foot there, now lower your hips…"

*　　　*　　　*

"Pearl! Come sit with us!" Mike invited. Pearl had had a morning of training and had just dished herself lunch.

"Okay!" Pearl agreed. She went over to her friends and sat down.

"What were you guys doing?" Pearl Wielder inquired.

"I was doing my battle stance,' Pearl said.

"Water patrol," said Asher.

"Food patrol," said Mike.

"Helping Goat Jump with lunch," Lucas said. "He had me chopping onions."

"Poor you." Pearl Wielder said. "I was on building patrol. Leading it, actually."

"Good job," Mary congratulated her. "I was helping Magic Healer."

"When will Sundance and Moonlight be back, Pearl?" Mike asked.

"Hopefully in two days," Pearl responded.

"Wow, so soon." Asher said. "Do you think they will make the deadline?"

"Of course they will," said Pearl Wielder, elbowing Asher. "They did it for the other tasks, so why not this one? They even have longer to do it."

Pearl smiled. "Thanks."

"I'll be glad to see those two kitties again," Mary commented.

"Pearl!' Wolf Eye called.

"Coming!" she yelled back. "See you guys." She went over to Wolf Eye and Hawk Wing. A little while later, Asher joined them.

"We're getting water,' Wolf Eye said. "Come on."

"And we're off!' Asher yelled.

"Asher," Pearl groaned.

* * *

After getting the water, the patrol headed back, getting to camp just in time for supper. There was a trail now, so the going to and from the stream was quicker.

"Let the Rebels gather!' Viper Strike called.

Pearl looked at Wolf Eye, confused. Why a meeting? And why just before supper? Couldn't it wait till after? Pearl was starving.

"Today, I have a very special announcement," Viper Strike began. "We have gotten enough food and water to last us a long time, and now all patrols will be dedicated to building the new base. This work will include digging it out, spreading the dirt, chopping logs for supports, bringing the logs to the new base, putting the supports in place, and making the place comfy. The rooms we will have to dig out are the bunks, food and water storage, Magic Healer's workspace, Jewel Crafter's workspace, and later on, a small farm for mushrooms. Even later on we might make plumbing, but for now we will be getting our water and disposing of our waste the same way we have been doing. Hawk Wing, you will be in charge of organizing these patrols. Now, return to your duties."

Pearl's head was reeling. There was so much to be done! But before anything, Pearl needed dinner.

Chapter 23

It was the next day, and the deadline of the last task.

Just after lunch, Pearl was having a quick rest before work. Then, Viper Strike came up to her.

“I’m glad you found this base Pearl,” Viper Strike commented. “It's a good place.”

“Thanks Viper Strike!” Pearl said embarrassedly.

Viper Strike smiled. “By the way, you’re helping Magic Healer and Mary for the afternoon. Have fun!”

“I will!" Pearl said, and ran over to Magic Healer and Mary.

“Viper Strike said I'm helping you!” She said.

Magic Healer smiled. “That’s right. Come on, you two.”

* * *

Laughing, Pearl chased Mary through the trees, a bundle of herbs in her arms. “I’m going to catch you!” she yelled. “Just you wait!”

“Never!” Mary giggled, avoiding Pearl’s outstretched hand.

“Come on you guys,” Magic Healer called, smiling to herself. “Come help me gather this thyme.”

“Okay,” Mary said.

“Coming!” called Pearl.

Pearl and Mary ran over to Magic Healer.

“We’ll go back after this,” Magic Healer said. “We’ve gotten a lot.”

“Alright!” The two apprentices agreed.

After collecting the thyme, they headed back to camp, playing all the while.

They got to the camp, dropped off all of the herbs at the Magic Healer’s store, and went to get some dinner.

* * *

Pearl was panting. She had been hauling logs that were practically trees all afternoon, with only Mike as help. At first they had talked, but now they put all of their energy into the work. It was too exhausting to do anything else. It would be a long, long afternoon, with plenty of time to worry about the tasks. Would the lynxes be alright? Would they succeed or fail? Where were they? Were they alright? Were they hurt? Scared? What was happening to them? Pearl's mind drifted from worry to worry, not knowing what to think.

*　　　*　　　*

“Rest!’ Viper Strike called. Pearl sighed with relief. Even if she loved being a part of the Rebels, the work was sometimes hard, and this time was one of them. The only other time she could remember working this hard was rebuilding the old base when it flooded, during one of the biggest rain storms Pearl had ever seen. And even with all of the work, the base still seemed so far from finishing.

Pearl thought the war might be over before the base was finished, and that was saying something.

"Dinner!" Goat Jump hollered.

Pearl was glad it was time for dinner. She was hungry! She walked over to where an assortment of cattails, nuts, berries, and stewed squirrel meat was being served.

"Looks good," Pearl complemented Goat Jump.

"Thanks," Goat Jump said. "Hope you like it."

Pearl went over to Pearl Wielder and the apprentices, ready for a fun dinner break that might distract her from the tasks.

* * *

Pear was filled with a mixture of excitement, worry and dread. The deadline of the last task was coming up any hour, and her cats would hopefully be back any hour, too. What if they didn't have the file? What if they had the file but came too late? What if they didn't come at all? The only thing Pearl wished for was for the tasks to be over, but at the same time, she didn't want them to end in case her cats failed. She glanced at the sky. The sun was beginning its decent. Where were her cats? Worry after worry rushed through her head as the sun rushed toward the horizon.

Chapter 24

Pearl glanced at the sky. There was barely a speck of light left in it, and her cats were nowhere to be seen. Pearl was starting to think that her cats weren't coming back, that they were trapped somewhere and wouldn't make the deadline. Or maybe… they didn't want to come back? Pearl quickly pushed that thought to the back of her head. Of course her cats wanted to come back. They were her cats, after all. But then again…

* * *

The sun could barely be seen, and at times it looked like that sun had disappeared for good, but then Pearl would catch a glimpse of it, and a little hope would return to her. But even with the small glimpses of sun, Pearl was starting to realize that her cats might not be coming back.

*   *   *

The last few rays of sun were dipping over the horizon, and Pearl was sure her cats had failed. She felt like weeping. How would she be able to live without them?

"Pearl, look!" Asher shouted excitedly.

Pearl scowled. Didn't he see she was in no mood for games? "Asher, leave me-"

"Wait Pearl,' Asher interrupted. "Look in the forest. There's something moving!"

Pearl looked up, expecting to see a squirrel running by, or maybe a rabbit. But there weren't even those wildlife creatures, it seemed. The forest looked empty.

"I don't see anything Asher," she said. "Leave me be and stop messing with me."

"I'm not messing with you," Asher protested. Then, "Look! To your right!"

Pearl half-heartedly looked, wishing Asher would stop messing with her. "I don't-" she started. But then she looked again. And again. There was something moving.

Looking closer, Pearl saw that the first shadow she saw was accompanied by one more. Could it be? Pearl tried not to get her hopes up, telling herself that it could just be a doe and its fawn out for a walk. But Pearl ran for a closer look anyway.

As she was running, she looked up to see the sun was still casting a few feeble rays over the forest. It wasn't too late! If it was her cats, and if they had the file, then they had made the deadline and had finished the final task! But they depended on those two big ifs. Two very, very big ifs.

Then, she was at the shadows.

And the shadows were purring!

Pearl could barely believe it. Her cats were here! They had made the deadline! But did they have the file? Petting their heads, Pearl lowered herself down to the lynxes' level and looked at them.

At first it seemed that the cats had found no file, but then Pearl looked closer, at a scrap of something in Moonlight's mouth. She gently tugged at it, and Moonlight opened her mouth, allowing the parchment to fall from it into Pearl's hand. There were creases that Pearl opened, and saw that what had looked like a scrap of garbage was a blueprint for an elaborate structure! Pearl could only imagine what the building was used for. But that was for later. Right now, all of the Rebels needed to know that nothing could separate Pearl from her cats.

*   *   *

"Let the Rebels gather!"

Pearl had alerted Viper Strike of her cat's arrival and was ready to be done with the tasks, once and for all. Viper Strike only needed to make it official.

Then, Viper Strike began. "It is time for the finishing of the third and final task!"

Chapter 25

"The cats had one week," Viper Strike continued, "from sunrise on the first day until sunset on the seventh. They had to steal a file from under the nose of Adolf Hitler. This deadline has been met, although barely. The file, that the cats have retrieved, is now in Pearl's hands. Pearl, bring the file forward."

Pear carefully held the file in her hands and presented it to Viper Strike.

"The cats have retrieved this file and completed the third and final task successfully!' Viper Strike announced, holding the file aloft.

Pearl was elated with joy, and she could hear whoops and hollers from her friends.

Viper Strike waited for things to quiet down, then continued. "At the beginning of the tasks, I said if the cats completed all of the tasks, then not only would they become a trusted part of the Rebels, but Pearl would also earn her warrior name."

Pearl was happily surprised. In the worries of the tasks, she had completely forgotten about that!

"So," Viper Strike said. "At midday tomorrow, Pearl's warrior ceremony will take place. Wolf Eye, I would like to speak with you. The rest of the Rebels, return to your duties."

Wolf Eye followed Viper Strike away from the crowd of Rebels, and Pearl, excited for her warrior ceremony, went to tend to the needs of her tired cats.

* * *

"Let the Rebels gather!" Viper Strike called.

It was midday, and time for Pearl's warrior ceremony. Pearl didn't know if she had ever felt this excited. Her cats had successfully completed the tasks, and were at her side, standing erect with alertness, reacting to Pearl's excited mood.

Then, Viper Strike began. "There is one of the apprentices here that has completed their training."

Pearl could hardly wait to hear her warrior name!

"Thanks to their mentor," Viper Strike continued, "they have learned the arts of combat, survival, and the skill of their mentor. In this training, they have developed their own skill that has been seen and acknowledged, and they will get their warrior name based on that skill. Today, this apprentice will be made into a warrior, as they deserve. Pearl, come forward."

Pearl felt light with joy. This was the moment all Rebel apprentices look forward to, from the day they joined. And now, the moment was Pearl's. She could barely restrain herself from running forward and using her excited energy. Instead, she walked importantly towards Viper Strike.

"Pearl," said Viper Strike, "do you promise to protect the Rebels, even with your life, and put the Rebels above everything, using the skills you have been taught?"

"Pearl's eyes shone with excitement. "I do!"

"Then, by these words," Viper Strike said, "I give you your warrior name. Pearl, from this moment onward, you will be known as Cat Commander, after your skill of commanding your cats."

"Cat Commander! Cat Commander!" The Rebels cheered.

Pearl ran to her friends, ready to embrace her new role as a warrior, and her new warrior name, Cat Commander.

Chapter 26

The next day, Cat Commander ate breakfast with the apprentices and Pearl Wielder.

"You guys better listen to me, cause I'm a warrior!" Cat Commander joked.

"Bow before her majesty!" Asher laughed, dramatically falling to his knees.

"The great warrior of the forest!" Pearl Wielder said, with a flourish of her arms.

"You must obey my command!" Cat Commander laughed.

"The great, wonderful, Cat Commander!" Lucas joked.

"Command and commander are almost the same words!" Mike noticed.

"Huh?" Mary asked. "Where did that come from?"

"Pearl-Cat Commander ended her sentence with command, and Lucas ended his with commander!" Mike explained.

Pearl Wielder laughed. "Trust Mike to think of that!"

Cat Commander pretended to pout. “Can't we go back to me being the greatest?” she pretended to wine, barely keeping back her laughter.

“Very well,” Asher said fake-solemnly.

“Must we follow your every command?” Lucas asked.

‘And bring you a feast every day?” Mary teased.

“And squirrels for your cats?” Pearl Wielder joked.

“I think my cats would think I was punishing them if I didn't let them hunt,” Cat Commander said.

“Then I will take over the duty of eating them!” Asher laughed.

“No me!” Lucas teased.

“Not you two, it’s for me!” Mike laughingly protested.

“It’s not for any of you,” Cat Commander said. “It’s for me, the greatest warrior!”

Just then, Talon Claw walked by and overheard what Cat Commander said.

“When have you faced down armies?” Talon Claw asked. “What feats have you done? Youngsters these days are too full of themselves, if you ask me."

"Actually Talon Claw," Mike argued. "We fought in the battle in the clearing, P-Cat Commander found the new base, with help, and her cats finished the tasks successfully under her command."

"Youngsters talk back now?" Talon Claw grumbled. "When I was a kid, youngsters were taught proper manners and never talked back to their elders."

The kids could barely contain their laughter.

"Nothing to say to that, eh?" Talon Claw asked. "Guess I proved my point." With that, Talon Claw stalked away, and the kids erupted into laughter.

* * *

Wolf Eye, Viper Strike, and Hawk Wing were looking at the file Cat Commander's cats had found, while the rest of the Rebels worked on constructing the new base.

Cat Commander was leading her first patrol as a warrior, with Pearl Wielder and Mike. They were bringing chopped planks to the new base from various places in the nearby forest. The Rebels couldn't take all of their lumber from one place or the Nazis would see the disturbance, so Cat Commander's patrol was constantly going to different places to get their loads. On top of that, the planks were heavy, making it exhausting work.

“Lunch!” Goat Jump hollered to the building patrols. Cat Commander saw Mary and Magic Healer go off in different directions to go tell the plank chopping patrols.

“Finally,” Mike sighed. “That’s hard work!”

“Yah, my arms are dropping off,” Cat Commander complained.

“Mine too,” Pearl Wielder agreed.

They then loaded up their plates with food and found a place to sit, followed shortly after by the other kids. The kids on the chopping patrols had raced back, so they didn't take too long in joining them.

"I hate chopping logs," Asher announced.

"Just be glad you weren't hauling them," Pearl Wielder said.

"I got it off easy," Mary said. "I was sorting herbs!"

"Boy, I wish I could trade places with you," Mike said.

"Well I don't," disagreed Mary.

"Hey," Lucas said. "I wonder what will happen with the file Sundance and Moonlight got?"

"Yah," Cat Commander agreed. "I wonder if it's something important."

"I wonder if there will be a mission," Pearl Wielder wondered.

"Well if there is," Lucas commented, "I want to be on it."

"They wouldn't bring apprentices or new warriors," Mike said despondently. "They'd want experienced warriors with them."

"Yah, cause youngsters these days can't handle long travel," Asher mocked Talon Claw.

"Don't let him hear you," Mary warned.

"I won't," Asher said confidently.

Just then, Vine Hang walked over to them. "You'd better eat up fast," he said. "Work's starting soon."

"Okay, thanks Vine Hang!" Pearl Wielder said.

Vine Hang nodded, and walked away. Then, the kids put their undivided attention on their food.

Chapter 27

Cat Commander was getting into bed after an afternoon of work and a good, although meager dinner. For work, she had been hauling logs to the chopping patrols, who would then make the logs into planks. It was exhausting work, and was even harder than hauling planks. Cat Commander lay down, ready to have a rest, and recover.

"Goodnight Sundance, goodnight Moonlight," Cat Commander called softly to her cats.

"Meow."

"Mew."

*　　　*　　　*

The next day, Cat Commander had just finished eating lunch with her friends and was about to go to Hawk Wing to get her place in a patrol, when Viper Strike called a meeting.

"Let the Rebels gather!"
Cat Commander was sure it was about the file. Maybe the senior warriors had decided what to do about it!

"My senior warriors and I," Viper Strike started, "have decided what to do with the information enclosed in the file found by Cat Commander's cats."

Cat Commander was right!

"This file contains information of an outpost of Nazis two months' march from here. This outpost contains many resources that can be used for rebellion, as well as for food. However, this will be a hard outpost to take over, so Magic Healer and every warrior except one will go. For their safety, all apprentices will remain at the camp and continue building the base. Pearl Wielder, you will supervise them. Cat Commander, because it was your cats who found the file, you will join us if you wish."

"Of course!" Cat Commander agreed excitedly.

"Good. We will leave in a week. Wolf Eye is in charge of organizing supplies for the journey. Now, return to your duties."

Cat Commander was ecstatic. She was going with the warriors! On a mission for the information on the file her cats had found!

She went to Wolf Eye to see how she could help with the preparations that would take place in the following week.

* * *

The week flew by. Before Cat Commander knew it, it was time to say goodbye to the apprentices and Pearl Wielder, and start the journey. Everyone ran around, calling farewells and last-minute advice. Then, it was time.

"Let the Rebels gather!" Viper Strike called over the noise of the farewells. Slowly, the camp grew silent. Then, Viper Strike started. "It is time for those on the mission to leave. To those staying, I give these instructions. Do not stray far, only leave the camp to find food, building materials and water; keep up your guard; don't let any trace of your presence be visible, and keep building the base. I hope to find it almost completed by the time we come back. Remember, we will be gone for over four and a half months. Pearl Wielder, you are in charge. Now, let us be off!"

Cat Commander waved goodbye to her friends one last time, then they were off. The mission had begun.

* * *

The first month passed slowly, each day clawing by. Cat Commander had scratches everywhere from prickly brush, and the whole patrol stank. Luckily, they weren't low on food, thanks to Wolf Eye's calculations, but Cat Commander was getting bored of canned goods.

Walking near to the back of the patrol, Cat Commander wondered what the apprentices and Pearl Wielder were doing. Working on the base probably. Or maybe they were lounging around after a meal, wondering about Cat Commander and the warriors. Maybe they were…

"Halt!" Viper Strike called out.

Cat Commander jolted out of her daydreaming. Why had they stopped? They had just eaten lunch, and there was no reason for a rest, as far as Cat Commander could see.

Straining to see the front of the patrol, Cat Commander made out that Viper Strike was talking to someone! The person looked small, so they were probably young, apprentice aged. But Viper Strike couldn't be thinking of recruiting them, not now! They were in the middle of a dangerous patrol. Not that Cat Commander would mind the company, though. She was getting lonely, as the only young person on the patrol. As Talon Claw would say, ‘youngsters these days can't stand grown company, they think that they must have youngster company. Back in my day, youngsters knew that grown-ups are fun, but not now.’ Cat Commander silently laughed at the thought. Talon Claw was always calling out on the kids' manners.

“Let the Rebels gather!” Viper Strike said the customary call, but didn't really need to. All of the patrol, Cat Commander included, were already clustered around her. “This is Emily,” Viper Strike began, gesturing to the person she had been talking to. “I have checked her over for bugs, but Cat Commander, could you send your cats to check the surrounding area? If all is clear, then Emily will be traveling with us.”

Cat Commander quickly told her cats to do as Viper Strike said, and an hour later they came back, signaling to her that it was safe.

In that hour, Cat Commander and Emily got to know each other. Cat Commander told Emily all about the Rebels, the lynxes, the tasks, and all of the other things that she thought Emily might need to know.

Emily told Cat Commander that she was orphaned, and imprisoned in a facility where Nazis who were called doctors ran horrible tests on kids. Cat Commander was horrified at that. Luckily, Emily had escaped, and had survived in the wild until the Rebels had found her.

“Move on!” Viper Strike called.

Cat Commander sighed. It would be more fun with Emily there, but she was still going to be very bored.

*　　　*　　　*

The last month had passed. Cat Commander and Emily had talked and had figured out that the testing facility was close to the outpost that the warriors were attacking. After talking with Viper Strike, they decided to save some of the kids from the facility, on the conditions that only Emily, Cat Commander, Sundance, and Moonlight would be on the patrol, and they would abandon the mission after two days' time, no matter what. They would meet at the hidden tree that the Rebels were camping at, first at sunrise on the second day, then if either of the patrols didn't show up, at midday, then sunset if either patrol didn't show up again. If either of the patrols didn't show up at sunset, then something had gone wrong, and a rescue patrol was needed.

The Rebels had eaten an early breakfast, and after reviewing the conditions one last time, the two patrols parted, the main patrol to attack, Cat Commander's patrol to save.

Chapter 28

After a little while of travel, Cat Commander's patrol came to a large, rectangular building with no windows and only two doors, which were heavily guarded. Luckily, Emily knew the guard schedule, and while the guards were changing shifts, the saving patrol could slip inside. After a bit of waiting, they did just that.

But that was just the beginning, the easy part of the mission. Now, they had to avoid all soldiers and 'doctors', who would certainly know those on the saving patrol were trespassers. Then, they would have to get into the wards, which were even more heavily guarded than the front doors. Cat Commander hoped that Emily knew that guard schedule really well, because if she didn't, and they tried to slip in at the wrong time, they were goners.

*   *   *

It was a tedious task, getting into the wards. They had to creep along during the brief periods that the 'doctors' and soldiers weren't patrolling the sparkling white corridors, and quickly hide behind something when they heard footsteps. Luckily, there was lots of furniture. Fake plants, sofas, desks. Finally, they reached the doors, which were, as Emily had said, very heavily guarded. So how to sneak in?

Cat Commander had just the plan. She quietly whispered her plan to Emily, who liked it, then to her cats. Immediately, the two lynxes slunk off, and started meowing after they were a safe distance from Cat Commander and Emily.

That caught the guards' attention. Yelling, they ran after the cats, who picked up the pace, easily out running the guards.

Under the cover of the cats' distraction, the two remaining members of the saving patrol quietly opened the door that led into the wards, and slipped inside.

*　　　*　　　*

Inside the wards was a sharp contrast to the gleaming white of the corridors before it. It was filled with filth and grime in every corner, and the place stank like a bathroom which hadn't been washed in ten years. Cat Commander nearly puked. But they had a deadline, so Emily and Cat Commander searched around the filthy halls, looking for ‘patients’. Then, they heard noises in the next corridor. Cautiously, Cat Commander peaked around it.

And stared in horror.

In the room, ‘doctors’ were jabbing needles into the kids! The ‘patients’ cries were muffled by clothes wrapped around their faces. Looking away from the horror that was around the corner, Cat Commander mouthed, “What should we do?”

Emily mouthed back, “find a place to hide, then wait for them to come out and pull aside some kids that don't look too far gone.”

“Got it.”

They huddled behind a grimy wooden bench that looked big enough to hide a few kids. Waiting, Emily peered out of their hiding spot, while Cat Commander figured out how to make it fit more kids. The more they saved, the better.

Then, Emily popped her head back in and said, “their coming.”

Cat Commander peaked her head out ever so slightly and saw that sure enough, the ‘patients’ were coming, escorted by soldiers and ‘doctors’ on either end of the procession.

Cat Commander and Emily looked at each ‘patient’ closely, looking for the most alive ones. Then, Emily's hands shot out, one clamping around a boy’s mouth and another pulling him in. Emily whispered to the boy to be silent, and the boy fearfully nodded. Seeing his fear, Cat Commander gave him a whispered explanation. By the time she had finished, Emily had pulled in three more kids, and Cat Commander had to repeat the explanation again. When she had finished, the ‘patients’ and workers had disappeared.

"What are your names?' Emily asked.

"Matt," the first boy answered.

"Alison."

"Ashley."

"Drake.'

"Nice names," Cat Commander said kindly. Emily and Cat Commander didn't have to share their names, because Cat Commander had already shared them in the explanation.

"Come on," Emily whispered. "We've gotta get out of here."

They followed her back through the maze of corridors, following the same route they took on the way in. But, at the doors that led out of the ward, they were stuck. Emily and Cat Commander had used the lynxes to distract the guards on the way in, but how to get out without them? And hearing the padding of at least eight feet on the other side of the windowless doors, they knew it was heavily guarded. It seemed that their mission, that was going so well, had well and truly failed.

Chapter 29

One of the doors slowly creaked open. All of the kids shivered with fright. There was no other escape except through those doors, and if they ran, their footsteps would echo and send off red flags of their location. So they were trapped. Any moment, a barrel of a gun might poke it's snout through the opening. It would fire and…

One of the kids gave a shout of surprise that was quickly muffled. A snout was poking through the door, as they had thought, but it wasn't a gun snout. It was one of an animal! Then, a head of a Eurasian lynx squeezed through the gap made by the snout before it.

"Moonlight!" Cat Commander called softly with delight, and ran forward to hug the cat. "You saved us once again!"

Propping the door open, Cat Commander made way for the kids to follow the cats out of the wards, making them one step closer to freedom.

✳ ✳ ✳

The kids, followed by Sundance and Moonlight, had escaped the facility without any further trouble, and were headed to the meeting tree. It was already midmorning on the second day, so they had missed the sunrise meeting, but the midday meeting was still to come, so Cat Commander wasn't worried. It would just be another couple hours, then they would be on their way with the rest of the warriors, with supplies to show for their adventures, and five new apprentices that would be readily accepted by the Rebels, Cat Commander was sure. Then, they reached the meeting tree, and settled down to wait.

✳ ✳ ✳

The sun had reached its peak, proclaiming it to be midday, but no Rebels were to be seen. But Cat Commander wasn't too worried. A warrior would come at sunset, she was sure. In the meantime, she would get to know the kids they rescued.

*   *   *

The kids, it turned out, all had similar stories to Emily. Orphaned, they were put into the facility, and stayed there until they were rescued. They all had been orphaned fairly recently, after Emily had escaped, so the drugs had not done much damage.

Matt's stomach growled. "Anyone have any lunch?" he asked.

"Yah," Emily said. "Just a sec." she rummaged through her bag and produced some food. "Here it is. Dig in everyone!"

They each took their share of the food, and chowed down. After they finished, Cat Commander glanced at the sun. It was nearing sunset. "A warrior should be here soon," she announced.

"Cool!" Drake said. "I'm looking forward to meeting all these warriors you've been telling us about."

“I want to meet Talon Claw,” Alison said. “See how bad he really is. I bet you guys are just exaggerating.”

“We’re not!” Cat Commander protested. “You really shouldn’t want to meet him! He’s a full on grump! Always telling us kids off about the littlest things!”

“Yah,” Emily agreed. “Trust me, he’s the worst. Always going on about ‘back in his day,’ and how ‘youngsters these days don't have proper manners.’”

“Wolf Eye’s great though!” Cat Commander said.

“Of course you would say that,” Emily laughed. “He’s your mentor!”

“What’s a mentor?” Ashley asked. The definition of a mentor had not made it into Cat Commander’s rushed explanation in the facility.

Cat Commander launched into the definition of a mentor, and by the time she had finished, it was sunset. Cat Commander was starting to glance around expectantly, sure that a warrior would appear any minute.

“A warrior should be here soon!” she proclaimed.

“Finally,” Matt sighed. “It’s been ages.”

“Are we that boring to you?” Ashley teased.

“Kind of,” Matt said with a wink.

“How dare you!” Ashley cried, putting a hand to her heart.

“Hey, can we eat?” Drake interrupted. “I’m hungry.”

“Me too,” Alison agreed.

“Well, it’s about dinner time anyways,” Emily agreed also. “Here you go.”

She brought out some food, which they devoured hungrily. By the time they had finished, the sun was gone, but no warrior was in sight.

Chapter 30

Maybe the warriors were just late, Cat Commander comforted herself. Maybe they were just delayed and would be arriving soon. But an hour after sunset, she had to face the truth. Something had happened to the warriors.

Faced with this realization, Cat Commander revealed it to the other kids.

"What should we do?" Ashley asked.

"Get them," Cat Commander said. "Set the warriors free!"

"How is that possible?" Drake asked. "If all those warriors couldn't break into the outpost, then how can you?"

"I would just be rescuing the warriors, not attacking the outpost," Cat Commander argued.

"But to save the warriors, you have to get in," Alison protested. "And to get in, you need to invade the outpost, and invading is the same as attacking. So sorry Cat Commander, but I am not going with you. I just got out of imprisonment."

"Yah, I agree." Drake said.

"Sorry Cat Commander, but I'm staying here," Ashley agreed.

"Yah," said Matt.

"It's okay," said Cat Commander despondently. "Emily?"

"Sorry, but no." Emily responded.

"I understand. It's risky."

"When will you leave?" Alison asked.

"In a minute," Cat Commander answered.

"So soon?" Ashley asked.

"I need to get the scope of the land," Cat Commander explained. "Besides, I need to get to the warriors as soon as possible. Who knows what's in store for them."

"But-" Emily protested.

""I'm going," Cat Commander interrupted. "No matter what you say, so don't waste your breath."

With that, she stormed into the night, her cats running after her.

✳ ✳ ✳

The outpost was gigantic, and there were soldiers everywhere. But Cat Commander had to get in. the warriors depended on her. Only her.

Despite what she had said earlier, she was mad at the others for deserting her. She and Emily had already done something dangerous together, so why chicken out from this mission? And the others- she and Emily had saved them from a terrible fate! Surely that counted for something! Surely they felt some debt to her! But, even as she thought this, Cat Commander knew it wasn't fair to resent the others for not coming. This mission was a thousand times more dangerous than breaking into the facility. Besides, she still had Sundance and Moonlight.

Cat Commander looked around. Seeing a good hiding spot, she went over to it and settled down, ready to watch the guard patterns.

*　　*　　*

Cat Commander felt something nudge her. She started. She had fallen asleep! Looking beside her, she saw Moonlight staring worriedly at her, the lynx's head outlined against the sunrise. Gazing into the outpost, Cat Commander saw prisoners being led out in chains, into a walled and guarded outdoor area. Looking closer, Cat Commander saw that the prisoners were the warriors! They had been captured.

Up until that point, Cat Commander hadn't really believed that something had happened to the warriors. But there was the evidence, right in front of her eyes. Scanning their faces, Cat Commander hoped desperately that none were missing, for it would mean that none had perished. They were all there, even Viper Strike, who, in the Nazi's eyes, had committed the worst offence, leading the Rebels. But what was happening to the warriors? Why were they out there, and not in their cells? Peering once again into the enclosed area, Cat Commander saw that the guards were tying the warriors on to stakes secured into the ground, which were spaced well, and evenly, apart. But why? Then, Cat Commander got her answer.

The crowd that had gathered was booing at the warriors, and throwing stones at them! The warriors could dodge a few, but most hit, and the hits looked like they hurt a lot. Cat Commander would have to move fast. She got out of her hiding spot, careful not to be seen, and went to observe the entranceway closer. Her cats followed, keeping to the shadows. With a sinking heart, Cat Commander saw that the entrance was guarded carefully, with a soldier to pat down everyone who wanted to enter. Another guard was looking at identification cards. There was no way in. Unless…

Chapter 31

Mayhem reigned. Cat Commander had sent her cats in while the guards were focused on checking over some people, and, as she had hoped, the guards had left their posts to help catch the cats. The lynxes were good at not getting caught.

During the confusion, Cat Commander slipped inside the outpost, and ran to the warriors.

“Viper Strike!” she called.

“Cat Commander!” Viper Strike said with surprise. “What are you doing here?”

“Rescuing you,” Cat Commander responded.

You can’t. There are too many guards. Sundance and Moonlight can't distract them forever.”

“But they can for a little while. Maybe if I-”

“Cat Commander, I speak to you as your leader when I say this. Leave us. If you get caught, then who will tell the Rebels at the base?”

"Emily-"

"Doesn't know the way. Only you do. Now go. I order you."

Cat Commander stared at Viper Strike, unwilling to leave her leader, her mentor, and the rest of the warriors. Finally, she turned to go.

"Wait."

Cat Commander turned around.

Viper Strike reached out a grimy hand that was filled with a small scrap of paper. "Take this."

Cat Commander took it, and made to open it up.

"Not now," Viper Strike warned. "Later. Now leave! I order you!"

Cat Commander nodded, too full of despair to respond. Then she ran away from the people that had taught her so much, the people that had given her hope, and who would never, ever, desert her. And now she was deserting them.

*   *   *

Cat Commander came to a stop, far away from the outpost, her lungs breathless and her heart beating wildly. Her cats lay down beside her. Then, Cat Commander opened the piece of paper Viper Strike had given her. It was filled with a poem.

"Take up our quarrel with the foe:
To you from failing hands we throw
The torch; be yours to hold it high.
If ye break faith with us who die
We shall not sleep, though poppies grow
In Flanders fields." *

*by John McCrae, 1915

About the Author

Elianna Wylie lives in Ontario, and loves to take walks on her city's nature trails. Besides writing, Elianna also likes to forage, read, explore the outdoors, and hang out with friends and family. As of now, The Rebels is the only book she has written, but she plans to continue the Freedom Isn't Free series. Some other books to watch out for are The Watchers, and Survivor Pack, which are separate novels.

Manufactured by Amazon.ca
Bolton, ON

24569364R00092